Student Depression

A Silent Crisis in Our Schools and Communities

Marcel Lebrun

Rowman & Littlefield Education
Lanham, Maryland • Toronto • Plymouth, UK
2007

Published in the United States of America
by Rowman & Littlefield Education
A Division of Rowman & Littlefield Publishers, Inc.
A wholly owned subsidiary of The Rowman & Littlefield Publishing Group, Inc.
4501 Forbes Boulevard, Suite 200, Lanham, Maryland 20706
www.rowmaneducation.com

Estover Road
Plymouth PL6 7PY
United Kingdom

British Library Cataloguing in Publication Information Available

Library of Congress Cataloging-in-Publication Data

Lebrun, Marcel.
Student depression : a silent crisis in our schools and communities / Marcel Lebrun.
p. cm.
Includes bibliographical references.
ISBN-13: 978-1-57886-552-9 (hardcover : alk. paper)
ISBN-13: 978-1-57886-553-6 (pbk. : alk. paper)
ISBN-10: 1-57886-552-2 (hardcover : alk. paper)
ISBN-10: 1-57886-553-0 (pbk. : alk. paper)
1. Depression in children. 2. Depression in adolescence. I. Title.
RJ506.D4L425 2007
618.92'8527—dc22

2006027008

™ The paper used in this publication meets the minimum requirements of American National Standard for Information Sciences—Permanence of Paper for Printed Library Materials, ANSI/NISO Z39.48-1992.
Manufactured in the United States of America.

To all the students with whom I have worked
over the last 27 years of teaching.
I want to thank them for teaching me about
uniqueness and exceptionalities
and that every child deserves to be treated
in a way that meets his or her needs, not mine.

Contents

Preface

Student Depression: A Silent Crisis in Our Schools and Communities was written to serve as a guide to educators who deal with depression in the classroom. It is my hope that the solutions in this work will promote an increased awareness and sensitivity to the issues surrounding childhood and adolescent depression. This resource is a compilation of a variety of ideas and strategies I have learned throughout my 27 years of teaching in the private, public, and higher education systems.

I became interested in depression in 1992 when I was exploring topics for my doctoral dissertation. I was presented with an exceptionally difficult student that year in my fifth-grade class. Jonathon had a series of issues around behavior: acting out with severe aggression, bullying, withdrawal, isolation, and family and emotional baggage were prohibiting him from succeeding at school. I felt he had many positives but I could not reach him in a way that made a connection and impact on his school and home life. It was only years later that I recognized that many of his symptoms were directly related to depression. As a 10-year-old, Jonathon was severely depressed, with no one around to diagnose him or give him the appropriate help or programming he needed to be successful in middle school.

Since my time teaching Jonathon, I have continued to study depression. The field continues to intrigue me with all the new aspects that seem to manifest themselves in the new research. This disorder affects many individuals and its impact continues to be felt daily in the lives of individuals. Recently, in New Hampshire, a young man at the high school level committed suicide. His depression was never identified and, therefore, never addressed, and a young life was cut short. It is easy to say, "If he had told us he was depressed, we could have helped him." Often, children or adolescents do not know that they are depressed. They just feel bad. If they say something about it they can be accused of being lazy, unmotivated, or whiney. They are children and therefore need to act like children. They are not mini-adults born with all the necessary brain power to solve complex problems or to make connections between emotions and behavioral actions. It is only in teaching and giving permission to children to share their feelings and multitude of emotions that we can guide them with specific problem-solving strategies that they can integrate into their repertoire of skills. It is with specific guidance that we empower them to become individuals who have a sense of power, rather than a sense of powerlessness, hopelessness, and helplessness.

Children today have a keener source of awareness as they seem to be less sheltered and naïve as previous generations. They are asked to deal with many social issues long before they have the power to understand the components or the implications of these issues. They just know that they need to survive as best they can. For some children who are more vulnerable, their ability to withstand all the challenges of being abused, neglected, abandoned, rejected, isolated, hungry, threatened, or fearful are just too much to handle, and so begins the descent into a state in which they can become invisible, or self-destructive.

It is my hope that this book will serve as a guide for change. My goal is to help ensure that teachers everywhere do not miss the clues that children give every single day. It is time for the adults to help these children so that they can become psychologically healthy citizens.

It is only in acknowledging the problem that we can begin to truly define it in a way that will lead to effective change. It is very easy to say someone else needs to deal with these children. By passing the responsibility, we stand the chance of losing more children to suicide. In a later chapter, I address this issue and the surprising statistics.

As you read this book, keep an open mind. Ask yourself the tough questions: What can I do? How can I use my power? When can I help this child? How will I help this child develop the skills he or she needs to be successful? If I don't do something, then what? Can I live with myself if I do nothing? The one thing I try or do may save a life! Isn't every child worth the effort?

At times it is very difficult to comprehend the discomfort of depression because it seems unfathomable or unreasonable to those who do not suffer from it. Those who function at a relatively healthy level find that depressed children have a completely irrational view of the world. Many individuals think there are simple solutions for depression. This is due to the fact that many people truly do not understand the complexities of what childhood depression is and what it is not.

I encourage you to share this book with parents, colleagues, and students so that the world of depression may become less daunting, impacting all children positively.

Acknowledgments

Megan Brown, my wonderful graduate assistant at Plymouth State University, has been of great assistance in making this book a reality, as were the editors at Rowman & Littlefield Education. Profound thanks to all current and former colleagues for the inspiration, the guidance, and the support during the tough years as well as during the great years.

I want to thank my family and friends for all their encouragement and belief in my abilities and gifts. It has been through your support that I have been able to grow both personally and professionally. I thank you all for your guidance and assistance.

Chapter One

Introduction: Who Are These Individuals?

The word *depression* evokes a variety of responses in people. For some it is a personal experience that brings up emotions of dark places full of isolation and misery. The American Heritage Dictionary defines a depressed person as being low in spirits, dejected, and suffering from psychological depression. What exactly is psychological depression? It is the journeys into these far-away places within the mind that hold many anxieties and feelings of helplessness and worthlessness. For others, this word is a journey that they traveled alongside a significant other, a colleague, or a relative. Everyone has been touched by depression in some capacity. It is only now in the 21st century that we are beginning to truly understand the magnitude of its grasp and influence on the lives of the affected individuals.

Depression is an emotion that cannot be counted or measured. It is not an inability to feel joy, but rather feelings of helplessness or hopelessness, of irritation, and often, of anger. Depression is widely misunderstood, as there are a variety of myths as to its causation. The causes are discussed in detail in later chapters. The distinction between clinical depression and psychological depression must be very clear. Clinical depression is often caused by a chemical imbalance in the brain.

It is generally believed that depression is caused by the individual, who can turn it off at any time. Unfortunately, the reality of this disorder is much more complex in nature than just snapping out of it.

Mental-health professionals have spent many years in research and have created a variety of labels, diagnoses, and classification systems to identify children and adults with depressive disorders. The term *depressive disorder* implies that the person has a number of symptoms, including depressed mood to a profound degree, and have a functional impairment in their ability to carry out their everyday activities (Fitzpatrick & Sharry, 2004).

There is no such thing as a typical case of depression. It is not to be assumed that any two cases or individuals will manifest the disorder in the same way. Depression is too multileveled in intensity and complexity to be given a generic plan of action or treatment. Each case is as individual as the individual suffering from the disorder.

Depression in children has some commonality in symptomatology; however, the inability of children to articulate exactly what is causing the unhappiness or depression is to be expected. It is important to recognize that not all depression is manifested in depressive behaviors such as withdrawal or destructive acts toward oneself and others.

It is particularly difficult for children experiencing depression to be able to explain to adults what it is that they are living through or with. It becomes even more complex with teenagers who already feel a sense of alienation from adults. They often fear that by speaking out that they will be perceived as being incompetent, unbalanced, and dysfunctional. They also fear placement in settings that may limit their individuality or freedom. The price of speaking out is often seen as too high, so many suffer in silence, until an action or a behavior brings their depression to the forefront of their lives and/or impacts the lives of those around them.

Adolescent depression occurs in a time of emotional upheaval, raging hormones, great drama, and heightened sensitivity. It is a time when a child no longer believes he or she is a child, but a young adult who should have the freedom to make choices. It is a period of rebellion and experimentation, much to the frustration of the adults in their lives. The parents and significant adults in these children's lives characteristically have honorable intentions in protecting their children from harm. However, they will at times harness their child in such a way as to prevent this normal rebellion that is part of the defining of one's future identity. The child or adolescent begins to feel restricted both emotionally and physically. Thus begins the onset of feelings of anger, frustration, and helplessness that have all been identified as some root causes of depression.

Clinically depressed children signal their distress very differently than do adults. Children do not meet the criteria often used for adult diagnosis. Consequently, what is now identified as a biologically based mood disorder affecting two percent of children has largely been misdiagnosed or not diagnosed. Spotting depression requires a keen eye to the manifestations that depression will produce. Children express their depression in a variety of ways and in a variety of situations. The core symptom is not sadness, but irritability and aggressiveness. The mood disturbances can also manifest themselves in hidden and mysterious pains, such as headaches, gastrointestinal pain, and injuries that appear to have no obvious source. Accompanying these mysterious illnesses or aches is a noticeable drop in academic performance if the child is of school age, or a lack of motivation to learn new things, and/or lack of curiosity on the part of a toddler.

Another key indicator is the abruptness of behavior change: a social child, who is doing well, suddenly develops problems with peers and ignores schoolwork. The child becomes distant and seems socially withdrawn. The child seems to reject what he or she has sought out in the past. He or she no longer wants to participate in birthday parties, go on field trips, or play with friends, and often will reject invitations to do activities previously enjoyed. About the same time, the child begins to withdraw from his or her peers, and comes across as unresponsive to maintaining friendships. He or she becomes unwilling or unable to make the investment in the time to nurture friendships. Early detection and treatment are keys to preventing chronic depression and relapses.

Chapter Two

Depression Unmasked: Looking into Their Inner World

Some children and adolescents seem to be more predisposed toward depressive disorders than others. The list below is general and its contents are not to be used as diagnosis criteria for identification of a depressive child.

The emotionally sensitive child presents with a constellation of problems, indicators, and symptoms that cause much concern to the adults with whom he or she comes into contact at home and at school. Shaughnessy (1998) in New Mexico has done extensive research on emotionally sensitive adolescents and has created a list of criteria that may be used as a guide in identifying children who are more likely to develop depressive-like symptoms in their young lives.

The following list may be manifested in varying degrees and not present at all in some children. Several indicators have been documented and are common in many cases. The list has been adapted from Shaughnessy's work:

1. *Clinging behavior:* Manifested when a child has a perceived fear of abandonment or rejection. This behavior is often seen by children in the early years of life and will often disappear as the child ages and goes on to school or daycare. Clinging behavior is a concern because the emotional state of the child and the perceived fears that accompany this behavior may be manifested in a series of irrational thoughts and possible phobias that may lead to feelings of helplessness and/or poor self-esteem. For example, "Why is this person leaving me? Why don't they want me to come along? What is wrong with me? Am I not good enough?" Such thoughts may lead to a child becoming paranoid and, therefore, unable to see things in a rational way. As a result, it is possible that the seeds of depression could take root.

2. *Withdrawal:* For some children, it is better to avoid adults who do not understand or who cannot comprehend what they are experiencing. Thus, they prefer to be alone. The adolescent or child may think, "I can solve this on my own," or, "They don't understand," or "If I tell I will be in more trouble." The viable option they create is, "I can deal with this in my own way in my own world and no one needs to know." This withdrawn behavior is often seen by adults as part of the transition that many adolescents undergo in finding their identity. Since most parents want to respect their child's privacy, they do not invade the treasured space of a child's room. Withdrawal is a concern when the child stops wanting to interact with all aspects of his or her daily life, such as meals, family outings, and social functions. As a parent or teacher, being in the child's space will create conflict and will shake things up. Do not be afraid to advance as you are the adult and you need to give the message that withdrawing from life is not an option. The child or adolescent will perceive this as meddling or that you really care about what is going on with them. Keep them interactive.
3. *Shyness or inhibition:* When is being shy a problem? It becomes a difficulty when it impairs the daily functioning of the child. The child may refuse to participate in activities that would be of interest and typical for the age group. The child may also decline to become involved or risk participating for fear of failure or embarrassment.
4. *Repression:* The child or student finds it extremely difficult to express anger when appropriate or other emotions when reasonable to do so. The child would rather internalize all the hate, tension, anger, and frustration than to allow his or her family, peers, or tormentors to have it. He or she feels unworthy of allowing this emotion to come through. It is therefore buried deeply in a storage room of the subconscious, where it festers and begins to damage the whole being. The child is fearful that visible external anger will be reason for abandonment, shame, punishment, or the taking away of something precious. This irrational fear then becomes internalized to the detriment of the mental well-being of the child.
5. *Criticism:* The depressed child does not react well to criticism in any way. Despite the time, place, or situation, they will overreact or underreact. Those who overreact to any type of constructive feedback are seeing another component of how deficient they are as human beings.

"Why would I want someone to tell me that I am incompetent? I already know it." "I know that I am useless and cannot learn or apply new things quickly," is often the mind-set of the depressed child. Negative criticism is like a huge red F on a paper. It denotes that the individual is lacking and, therefore, unworthy. This sense of worthlessness ties in with low self-esteem. The perception of low self-esteem can be identified in many ways. At times, overcompensation, overreaction, and defensiveness are seen as reactions to the most trivial details or situations. For example, a child tearing up his or test because of several errors and possibly because someone has made a snide comment under their breath are the triggers for the reaction. The perception of others becomes a primary focus. To avoid appearing inferior, a depressed child may feel it is better to distract with an overreaction or a behavior that will draw away the spectators from the real root of the problem. The inability to accept criticism is like a match that is ready to strike. Eventually, after many tries, it will light and burn. Unfortunately, the burn is not only to the people around the individual, but the flame burns brightly within. This burning begins to fester and is often manifested in anger. Anger is an emotion that manifests itself in many covert ways. It will present itself as self-destructive behavior, as omissions, as overreactions, or as depression. One of the most common ways is depression, especially in females. Women or young females hold the belief that they are not allowed to show anger as their male counterparts do. They, therefore, internalize the feelings associated with anger. Years of this type of behavior lead to depression. It is crucial when looking at depression that anger be investigated as well. The action of criticism and the resultant perceptions may lead a person to anger, which lends itself to frustration. In turn, it may lead to feelings of hopelessness and helplessness, then repressed anger and depressive-like behaviors or symptoms.

6. *Self-deprecation:* This behavior begins to manifest itself when the child or student begins to denigrate himself or herself with very negative statements. "I'm stupid! I am dumb! I'll never be able to do that! I give up! No matter what I do I will fail, so why try?" As a parent or teacher, be alert to these kinds of statements. The child is unable to recognize any of his or her positive qualities or strengths. The child is unwilling to believe or admit that he or she has abilities. As far as the

child is concerned, he or she fails at everything. This inability to accept positive praise is a warning sign that needs to be addressed with positive and direct intervention.

7. *Low self-esteem and low self-worth:* The student or child is in a mindset that he or she is at the bottom of the value continuum, unable to understand that he or she is a contributing member of a classroom or a family. The child's perceptions are that he or she has nothing to offer and is worthless, often using statements such as, "Why would you want to spend time with me? I am a downer. I am negative." These statements serve to push people away. Having people stay away confirms to the child that he or she is worthless. It is almost a confirmation that the beliefs the child had about himself or herself were true after all.
8. *Inability to forgive self or others:* One of the key issues in treating depression is the ability to forgive oneself and others. Sufferers obsess on their mistakes and shortcomings. A child will be unable to forgive an action by an adult that happened years earlier. The child harbors anger and frustration with ferocity. The child clothes himself or herself in this negativity and uses it to fuel his or her anger. This can be best illustrated with children whose parents divorce. The child becomes unable to forgive one parent, or their perception of who the "bad" parent is, and stays angry for years at that individual. The child is unable to get past the hurt of the situation. This provides a fuel line toward depression, and maintains it for decades. At times, individuals who perceive themselves as less than perfect do not learn from their mistakes but use the mistakes to admonish themselves and sabotage their efforts at new endeavors. They know they will fail and in so doing cannot forgive people who may have blocked or prevented them from accomplishing their task or mission. The inability to accept responsibility for choices, or having limited control in a situation, enriches the possibility that someone else will be credited with the blame. In many instances, the child or student puts up a wall or a front to the adult and will not allow that adult to interact or get past the barrier. This lets the adult know that the child has made a choice and that choice is not to respond or acknowledge the adult's wishes or demands. It is an immature behavior mastered early in development, but one that seems to carry into adulthood. The "silent treatment" is practiced frequently by depressed children and adults. It is so much easier to curl up and shut out the world.

No matter what the outside world says or does, it cannot penetrate the walls that surround the depressed child or student.

9. *Explosive emotional volatility:* Some students and children become the opposite of the closed, withdrawn child. They become explosively angry, and, at times, a danger to themselves and others. They will erupt in anger over the smallest detail or incident. Some may wait for that extra little provocation that will lead to an expression of extreme anger toward a teacher or parent who is seen as contributing to their difficulties or frustrations. Many educators and parents have failed over the years to see the connection between bullying and depression. The myth is that all children who are exhibiting depressive-like symptoms are withdrawn, isolated, or weak. As research has improved in this area, direct correlations have been made between violent behavior and depression. The anger and violence are just symptoms of depression. Some choose to withdraw, while others choose deadly force. The underlying motivation for the action is still depression. We have to be aware that depression can be manifested in multiple ways. No longer should we only pay attention to the withdrawn child in the corner. We need to be concerned with the one punching, kicking, biting, spitting, and shooting.

Depression is clinically defined in several ways: major depression, dysthymia, bipolar, and cyclothymia. The symptoms of dysthymia are similar to those of depression but are not as severe and are usually longer lasting. Symptoms usually manifest every day or most days, and to receive a diagnosis, must be present for at least one year. Symptoms such as poor appetite, insomnia, low energy, inability to concentrate, and feelings of hopelessness are typical. In contrast to major depression, sleep disturbance, appetite and weight changes, and psychomotor symptoms are less common with dysthymia.

Bipolar disorder is difficult to diagnose in adolescents because it has varied symptoms. The younger the age at which depression first appears, the more likely bipolar illness is to develop. Bipolar is characterized by cycling moods of depression and mania, irrational elation, frenzied activity, excitability, or anger over a period of at least a year. It is often manifested in acting-out behaviors, risk taking, alcohol and drug use, and explosive aggressive behaviors. The symptoms of the illness vary greatly.

Some children have more rapid cycles that vary in intensity, frequency, and duration, and that lead to very short or nonexistent "normal" mood periods. Treatment and identification must be carefully monitored, especially in adolescents, because of the unpredictability of adolescents' moods and interactions with the world. A diagnosis should not be given before an extensive study is undertaken of all the aspects of the adolescents' lives and behaviors.

Cyclothymia is a milder form of bipolar disorder in which the person presents alternating periods of despair and joy, enthusiasm and discouragement, sleepiness and wakefulness, self-confidence and self-pitying, laughing and crying. The disorder is manifested for at least a year in adolescents, and symptom-free periods last no longer than eight weeks. Treatment is to be monitored carefully so as to ensure that the behaviors are not part of ordinary development phases. Accumulation of data of ongoing behaviors is the first step to understanding whether a depressive disorder is being manifested or is in evidence.

Chapter Three

Causes of Depression

The conversation on the causes of depression takes many different paths. The journey is an integrated network of causes and explanations. Is there one true answer for the cause of depression, or is it a multitude of sources that arrive at one source to manifest itself into a specific disorder? For many years, scientists and mental-health practitioners have been gathering knowledge-based evidence to find the root cause of depression. In this chapter, the discussion will focus on the main areas that have been highlighted as possible causes.

To understand the causes, we need to investigate some historical aspects. Before the 1960s and 1970s, people with mild depression were either mostly ignored or institutionalized. Most families, physicians, mental-health practitioners, and educators were not fully cognizant of the impact of the depression. Some were unsympathetic and entreated the individual, in essence, to stop complaining and live with it. It is also at this time that major revolutions were happening in the United States regarding civil rights, education, feminism, political upheaval, and war. In the 1970s, the more individuals expressed their anger, the less depressed they became. Suddenly, a correlation was made between anger and depression. It seemed that the lack of expression of emotion led to a repression that would sit with the individual until some level of toxicity developed, i.e., depression. When this new awareness was discovered, the evolution of many treatment plans and strategies emphasized that anger was good and natural and that by expressing it an individual could achieve emotional well-being and mental fitness. This was hailed as the new cure. However, there was a stumbling block to this new theory: No matter how much anger individuals expressed, they remained depressed. The "cure" was really but a piece of the larger puzzle.

Over the years, many practitioners have believed that the cause for chronic, mild depression is unresolved anger. The theory states that people will remain depressed because they face so many anger-inducing situations (such as stress, relationships, children, family, career, finances, money, medications, and sex) in their daily lives that they cannot seem to handle all of these situations. Often when they are dealing with one event or situation, two more arise as secondary issues. They are often unable to catch up and effectively deal with all of the stressors present.

History is a wonderful teacher because it provides us with a richness of examples that show that mild depression existed and was rooted in everyday lives. Those who worked in the sweatshops a century ago struggled with the need for survival, the abject poverty, and the horrendous working conditions in both cold and heat. The health ramifications, the early deaths, and the lack of advancement were all factors that would have contributed to an individual being depressed. The Great Depression of the 1930s was defined by starvation, unemployment, and the abandonment of home and family.

The African Americans have had an incredible journey throughout history. If we examined all of the many situations throughout the centuries we would see many causes of depression. Sufferers face slavery, oppression, violence, poverty, discrimination, prejudice, and murder, all valid reasons for depression.

The war widows of the 1940s were another group of individuals who suffered depression when they lost their partners and husbands to wars thousands of miles away. Homemakers in the 1940s and the 1950s were to be the perfect mothers and wives. Many experienced mental-health issues because of these unrealistic expectations. Depression seems to have affected females more often than males in history. One may surmise that the female gender has a predisposition to chronic depression because of many societal causes. The question needs to be asked, "Why is there so much chronic depression in our society today?"

We do not work in sweatshops. There is no huge economic depression, and generally most North Americans do not live in violent or dangerous neighborhoods, except in some of the larger urban centers. We do not fear losing loved ones, except in terror attacks, and that fear has seen a decrease over the years since the 9/11 disaster occurred. Bigotry and prejudice against women, African Americans, and sexual orientation, has been less severe than in the past but is still an ongoing concern.

Historians will view this generation as being consumed by income, work, and all the toys and luxuries. People in the United States and Canada simply overvalue work and play and undervalue rest. Current society is characterized by political correctness, ignoring our needs and wants, and tolerating a life of chronic depression because there does not seem to be a cure. We have become desensitized to our problems and living conditions. Our coworkers, bosses, spouses, relatives, and neighbors are all depressed so why not us? We are all angry about various issues, and it seems that we make depression seem necessary and normal at a time when it is not. Do we begin to re-examine our priorities and redefine what we want, who we are, and where we want to be in our lives? This would be a great beginning.

When investigating causes of depression, there needs to be a distinction between psychological and genetic-biological depression. Psychological depression is defined as feeling rejected, ignored, anger-repressed, powerless, helpless, and/or suicidal. Genetic-biology depression is a disorder of the chemistry within the brain, and is due to genetic predisposition in the DNA makeup of the individual. There are definite links between influences and social factors as a cause.

The key question concerning depression is why some people become depressed and others do not. Genetic factors do play a role in the predisposition of depression, however many of the symptoms often are manifested by environmental stressors rather than an entirely genetically determined condition. Genetic factors influence people's behavior and cognitive style, leading in turn to a tendency to respond to certain environmental factors by becoming depressed. The extent to which our behavior and, thus, our life experiences and life events (and, indeed, our interpretations of these) are genetically determined remains to be discovered (Zeman, 1996).

Inherited attributes may contribute to vulnerability and depression through influences on people's exposure to environmental factors. The effects on choices and those of partners, friends, and lifestyles may also influence the development of depression. Childhood adversity and unprocessed early trauma (such as sexual abuse or any type of abuse) may also predispose the child or individual to depression. The involvement of economic circumstances that influence nutrition, safety, housing, and poverty, and exposure to threatening events or situations will predispose both parent and child to depression. The presence of poverty and deprivation worsen interpersonal relationships, which in turn leads to depression.

Depression in children, with its unique set of social and environmental factors occurring at this period of development, has created many puzzles for scientists and the medical profession. There are no clear answers as to whether the depression is caused by biological determinants or the influence of developmental factors. Social and interpersonal factors seem to be at the top of the list for common cause explanations. The list may include death or serious illness of a friend or family member, loss of love or attention from a friend or family member, breakup of a romantic relationship no matter how young the individual is, family problems, parental divorce, isolation/loneliness, rejection or teasing, physical, verbal or sexual abuse, substance abuse, hospitalization, especially for a chronic illness, trauma or disaster, stress, and all other life-altering situations. This list is not intended to be exhaustive.

In conclusion, the causes seem to be many, diverse, and multilayered in their interaction leading to childhood and adolescent depression episodes and illness. The key is to combine many pieces of the puzzle and become an astute child/student detective who is able to see the interconnectedness between factors, influences, and life events. It is only by combining the information from all sources that we may be certain to understand the complexities that exist within this disorder.

Chapter Four

Observations, Symptoms, and Checklists

This chapter comprises checklists that may guide your observations of the children with whom you work. These checklists can be used as a measure to confirm or discount the possibility that depression may be present. These lists are not intended as replacements for a physician's diagnosis or treatment plan.

Parents and teachers are on the front line when it comes to recognizing the manifestations of depression. Often, a child will receive excellent care and attention because of an overzealous teacher or parent who will not give up on the child no matter how rude or standoffish the child is. The adult is keenly aware of the existence of a potential problem and will search out answers and/or seek professional help through collaboration with other educators or mental-health professionals.

These checklists were adapted from those developed by the National Institute of Mental Health as a way of helping teachers and parents to identify a variety of symptoms.

The focus is on the four general areas of depressive disorders: major depression in children and adolescents, early-onset bipolar disorder (often seen as manic-depression), and bipolar disorder in adolescence.

Please observe on several occasions, collect data from multiple sources, and also document over time. These checklists are meant to be guides in your process. They must never be used to diagnose. It is hoped that they may be effective in helping the adult or parent document and recognize patterns that may be in existence or that are developing.

Checklist 4.1. Major Depression in Children

Name: ______________________________ Date: ____________________

Observer: ____________________________ Time: ____________________

Answer criteria: Circle yes or no for each criterion/symptom if it has been observed for the categories shown in the box below.

Abbreviate (F) for Frequency, (D) Duration, (I) Intensity

Frequency	Duration	Intensity
(a) Every 5 min.	(a) 5 min.	(a) Mild
(b) Every 15 min.	(b) 15 min.	(b) Average
(c) Hourly	(c) 30 min.	(c) Extreme
(d) Daily	(d) More than 30 min.	
(e) Too frequent to count	(e) More than 1 hour	

1. Displays irritability	Yes	No	(F)____	(D)____	(I)____
2. Displays aggressiveness	Yes	No	(F)____	(D)____	(I)____
3. Displays combativeness	Yes	No	(F)____	(D)____	(I)____
4. Feels angry all the time	Yes	No	(F)____	(D)____	(I)____
5. Seems sullen	Yes	No	(F)____	(D)____	(I)____
6. Complains about headaches	Yes	No	(F)____	(D)____	(I)____
7. Complains about stomachaches	Yes	No	(F)____	(D)____	(I)____
8. Experiences drop in grades	Yes	No	(F)____	(D)____	(I)____
9. Refuses to do homework	Yes	No	(F)____	(D)____	(I)____
10. Refuses to attend school	Yes	No	(F)____	(D)____	(I)____
11. Feels extreme anxiety about tests	Yes	No	(F)____	(D)____	(I)____
12. Has developed negative self-judgments	Yes	No	(F)____	(D)____	(I)____
13. Is down on himself or herself	Yes	No	(F)____	(D)____	(I)____
14. Believes her or she is weird and ugly	Yes	No	(F)____	(D)____	(I)____
15. Is picked on by others	Yes	No	(F)____	(D)____	(I)____
16. Has thoughts of death	Yes	No	(F)____	(D)____	(I)____
17. Is hypersensitive to criticism	Yes	No	(F)____	(D)____	(I)____
18. Overreacts to disappointment and frustration	Yes	No	(F)____	(D)____	(I)____
19. Becomes tearful	Yes	No	(F)____	(D)____	(I)____
20. Gives up easily	Yes	No	(F)____	(D)____	(I)____
21. Is unable to have fun	Yes	No	(F)____	(D)____	(I)____
22. Is withdrawn	Yes	No	(F)____	(D)____	(I)____
23. Mopes	Yes	No	(F)____	(D)____	(I)____

(*continued*)

Checklist 4.1. Major Depression in Children (*continued*)

24. Is not involved in activities	Yes	No	(F)____	(D)____	(I)____
25. Becomes lethargic	Yes	No	(F)____	(D)____	(I)____
26. Is apathetic	Yes	No	(F)____	(D)____	(I)____
27. Is dispirited	Yes	No	(F)____	(D)____	(I)____
28. Has difficulty sleeping	Yes	No	(F)____	(D)____	(I)____
29. Oversleeps	Yes	No	(F)____	(D)____	(I)____
30. Can't get up in the morning	Yes	No	(F)____	(D)____	(I)____
31. Sleeps in school	Yes	No	(F)____	(D)____	(I)____
32. Hallucinates	Yes	No	(F)____	(D)____	(I)____
33. Has delusions	Yes	No	(F)____	(D)____	(I)____
34. Is paranoid	Yes	No	(F)____	(D)____	(I)____
35. Puts on a good face in public and displays symptoms at home	Yes	No	(F)____	(D)____	(I)____

Source: Adapted from National Institute of Mental Health, 2005.

ANALYSIS OF RESULTS

When analyzing the results of this checklist, put a clear perspective on the evidence that the data have provided. Under no circumstances should emotion cloud your objectivity.

The essential feature of the major depressive episode is that there is a period of at least two weeks during which there is either depressed mood (as indicated by the categories listed above), or the loss of interest or pleasure in nearly all activities. The individual must experience at least 10–12 of these symptoms. The symptoms must persist for most of the day, nearly every day, for at least two consecutive weeks. A clinical interview is highly recommended to assess the child's state of being. Once the symptoms have been identified by the checklist, the assessor must find supportive evidence that shows that the symptoms cause clinically significant distress or impairment in social, school, or other important areas of functioning. When interpreting the data, ensure that the symptoms are not due to the direct physiological effects of a substance (e.g., drugs, alcohol, or medications). Particular attention must be paid to the fact that the child has suffered a loss and is in the process of grieving at the time of the assessment.

Checklist 4.2. Major Depression in Adolescence

Name: ______________________ Date: ______________

Observer: ____________________ Time: ______________

Answer criteria: Circle yes or no for each criterion/symptom if it has been observed for the categories shown in the box below.

Abbreviate (F) for Frequency, (D) Duration, (I) Intensity

Frequency	Duration	Intensity
(a) Every 5 min.	(a) 5 min.	(a) Mild
(b) Every 15 min.	(b) 15 min.	(b) Average
(c) Hourly	(c) 30 min.	(c) Extreme
(d) Daily	(d) More than 30 min.	
(e) Too frequent to count	(e) More than 1 hour	

1. Feels sad	Yes	No	(F)____	(D)____	(I)____
2. Feels hopeless	Yes	No	(F)____	(D)____	(I)____
3. Feels empty	Yes	No	(F)____	(D)____	(I)____
4. Cries in class	Yes	No	(F)____	(D)____	(I)____
5. Appears lethargic	Yes	No	(F)____	(D)____	(I)____
6. Moves slowly	Yes	No	(F)____	(D)____	(I)____
7. Seems sleepy	Yes	No	(F)____	(D)____	(I)____
8. Is unable to control hyperactivity	Yes	No	(F)____	(D)____	(I)____
9. Is extremely sensitive in interpersonal relationships	Yes	No	(F)____	(D)____	(I)____
10. Is highly reactive to rejection	Yes	No	(F)____	(D)____	(I)____
11. Is highly reactive to criticism	Yes	No	(F)____	(D)____	(I)____
12. Drops friends that are in conflict with him or her	Yes	No	(F)____	(D)____	(I)____
13. Is grouchy	Yes	No	(F)____	(D)____	(I)____
14. Prefers to sulk and cannot be cajoled into a better mood	Yes	No	(F)____	(D)____	(I)____
15. Overacts to disappointment or failure	Yes	No	(F)____	(D)____	(I)____
16. Takes months to recover from setbacks	Yes	No	(F)____	(D)____	(I)____
17. Feels restless and aggressive	Yes	No	(F)____	(D)____	(I)____
18. Becomes antisocial:					
• lies to parents	Yes	No	(F)____	(D)____	(I)____
• cuts school	Yes	No	(F)____	(D)____	(I)____
• shoplifts	Yes	No	(F)____	(D)____	(I)____

(continued)

Checklist 4.2. Major Depression in Adolescence (*continued*)

19. Believes he or she is different	Yes	No	(F)____	(D)____	(I)____
20. Believes no one understands him or her	Yes	No	(F)____	(D)____	(I)____
21. Believes everyone looks down on him or her	Yes	No	(F)____	(D)____	(I)____
22. Is isolated from:					
• family	Yes	No	(F)____	(D)____	(I)____
• schoolmates	Yes	No	(F)____	(D)____	(I)____
23. Finds a new mainstream of friends and peer groups	Yes	No	(F)____	(D)____	(I)____
24. Hangs out exclusively with one friend	Yes	No	(F)____	(D)____	(I)____
25. Becomes self-destructive	Yes	No	(F)____	(D)____	(I)____
26. Self-medicates with drugs or alcohol	Yes	No	(F)____	(D)____	(I)____
27. Stops caring about his or her appearance	Yes	No	(F)____	(D)____	(I)____
28. Regularly has morbid imaginings and thoughts of death	Yes	No	(F)____	(D)____	(I)____

Source: Adapted from National Institute of Mental Health, 2005.

ANALYSIS OF RESULTS

Much of the analysis is the same as previously noted in the childhood checklist. The key components in the adolescent depression checklist are the influences of social network, peer group, school success or failure, parental involvement, and self-esteem issues and/or development.

Symptoms of a major depressive episode usually develop over days and weeks. The depressive episode may be preceded by major anxiety symptoms that may last for weeks or months before the onset of the major depressive episode. The depressive episode typically lasts six months or longer, regardless of age of onset. If treated early, there is a total remission of symptoms and return to regular functioning. One of the main concerns about adolescents is their ability to magnify their problems, as many at that stage of their development do not have the proper brain development to accurately solve the problem without proper guidance. If left alone, many adolescents may slip into a depressive episode because they see no resolution to the problem or issue. Many adolescents do not have the strategies needed to effectively manage some of the stressors present in their young lives.

When interpreting the results found on this checklist, study all aspects of the adolescent's life and see which factors are presenting the challenging situations for the individual.

Checklist 4.3. Early-Onset Bipolar Disorder

Name: ______________________ Date: ______________

Observer: ______________________ Time: ______________

Answer criteria: Circle yes or no for each criterion/symptom if it has been observed for the categories shown in the box below.

Abbreviate (F) for Frequency, (D) Duration, (I) Intensity

Frequency	Duration	Intensity
(a) Every 5 min.	(a) 5 min.	(a) Mild
(b) Every 15 min.	(b) 15 min.	(b) Average
(c) Hourly	(c) 30 min.	(c) Extreme
(d) Daily	(d) More than 30 min.	
(e) Too frequent to count	(e) More than 1 hour	

Criterion/symptom					
1. Hair-trigger arousal system is set off by the slightest irritant or change	Yes	No	(F)____	(D)____	(I)____
2. Overreaction takes the form of:					
• irritability	Yes	No	(F)____	(D)____	(I)____
• opposition	Yes	No	(F)____	(D)____	(I)____
• negative behavior	Yes	No	(F)____	(D)____	(I)____
3. Has multiple mood shifts	Yes	No	(F)____	(D)____	(I)____
4. Acts like two different people (angel/devil)	Yes	No	(F)____	(D)____	(I)____
5. Controls rage in school	Yes	No	(F)____	(D)____	(I)____
6. Does not control rage at home	Yes	No	(F)____	(D)____	(I)____
7. Displays hyperactivity	Yes	No	(F)____	(D)____	(I)____
8. Is highly distractible	Yes	No	(F)____	(D)____	(I)____
9. Is inattentive	Yes	No	(F)____	(D)____	(I)____
10. Has decreased need for sleep	Yes	No	(F)____	(D)____	(I)____
11. Behaves in a grandiose manner	Yes	No	(F)____	(D)____	(I)____
12. Seeks control	Yes	No	(F)____	(D)____	(I)____

(continued)

Checklist 4.3. Early-Onset Bipolar Disorder (*continued*)

Item					
13. Is highly directive toward adults (bossy)	Yes	No	(F)____	(D)____	(I)____
14. Harasses other children/adults	Yes	No	(F)____	(D)____	(I)____
15. Has overt hypersexual activities and communicates them in the classroom	Yes	No	(F)____	(D)____	(I)____
16. Is greatly sensitive to heat	Yes	No	(F)____	(D)____	(I)____
17. Experiences insatiable craving for carbohydrates and sweets	Yes	No	(F)____	(D)____	(I)____
18. Experiences psychotic episodes of auditory hallucinations	Yes	No	(F)____	(D)____	(I)____
19. Experiences ragged sleep cycles	Yes	No	(F)____	(D)____	(I)____
20. Experiences night terrors	Yes	No	(F)____	(D)____	(I)____
21. Experiences violent nightmares	Yes	No	(F)____	(D)____	(I)____
22. Initially reacts to any request with no	Yes	No	(F)____	(D)____	(I)____
23. Experiences severe separation anxiety	Yes	No	(F)____	(D)____	(I)____
24. Refuses to attend school	Yes	No	(F)____	(D)____	(I)____
25. Has rages as seizures and:					
• is wild-eyed	Yes	No	(F)____	(D)____	(I)____
• has violent tantrums	Yes	No	(F)____	(D)____	(I)____
• kicks	Yes	No	(F)____	(D)____	(I)____
• hits	Yes	No	(F)____	(D)____	(I)____
• bites	Yes	No	(F)____	(D)____	(I)____
• screams	Yes	No	(F)____	(D)____	(I)____
• uses foul language	Yes	No	(F)____	(D)____	(I)____
• thrashes	Yes	No	(F)____	(D)____	(I)____
26. Experiences sleep disturbances	Yes	No	(F)____	(D)____	(I)____
27. Is difficult to rouse in the morning	Yes	No	(F)____	(D)____	(I)____
28. Gains energy throughout the day	Yes	No	(F)____	(D)____	(I)____
29. Is hyperactive (acts out) by the end of school day	Yes	No	(F)____	(D)____	(I)____
30. Reports extreme physical sensitivity to:					
• clothes	Yes	No	(F)____	(D)____	(I)____
• food	Yes	No	(F)____	(D)____	(I)____
31. Acts worse at home than school	Yes	No	(F)____	(D)____	(I)____

Source: Adapted from National Institute of Mental Health, 2005.

ANALYSIS OF RESULTS

This mood disorder may involve sharp swings from episodes of manic highs to periods of depressive lows or a mixed state in which manic energy combines with the depressed mood. When tabulating the results of this checklist, keep a clear perspective as to what kinds of symptoms are being manifested, and whether or not there is a predictable pattern to the episodes. In children, the scientific basis of this diagnosis is still evolving. Presently, there are two major components that are used most frequently in deciding whether bipolar disorder is present. Firstly, determine whether there is a family history of bipolar and, secondly, whether the symptoms exhibit a pattern unique to this age group. There is evidence to suggest that a form of pediatric mania is manifested in mood shifts that occur repeatedly throughout the day, and that the child has ultra-rapid mood cycling. Firstly, ensure that there are clear manifestations of the aggressive, unpredictable, oppositional, prolonged explosive rages one moment. Secondly, confirm that the upbeat mood changes go from silly, full of energy, and then back to destructive patterns.

Depressed children may be charming, humorous, intelligent, and verbally and artistically gifted. They may also be bossy, intrusive, insistent, and obnoxious. The key to proper identification and interpretation of these results is to see the connection between the variation in mood and acting-out behaviors.

Employ vigilance when interpreting the data from this measurement tool, as bipolar disorder in children may involve clusters of symptoms at various ages that resemble attention deficit hyperactivity disorder, oppositional defiance disorder, and conduct disorder. It is also important to note that these children should not be given stimulants or antidepressant medications that have been known to trigger manic and psychotic episodes.

Checklist 4.4. Bipolar Disorder in Adolescence

Name: ______________________ Date: ______________

Observer: ____________________ Time: ______________

Answer criteria: Circle yes or no for each criterion/symptom if it has been observed for the categories shown in the box below.

(continued)

Checklist 4.4. Bipolar Disorder in Adolescence (*continued*)

Abbreviate (F) for Frequency, (D) Duration, (I) Intensity

Frequency	Duration	Intensity
(a) Every 5 min.	(a) 5 min.	(a) Mild
(b) Every 15 min.	(b) 15 min.	(b) Average
(c) Hourly	(c) 30 min.	(c) Extreme
(d) Daily	(d) More than 30 min.	
(e) Too frequent to count	(e) More than 1 hour	

Manic phase

Item					
1. Has difficulty sleeping	Yes	No	(F)____	(D)____	(I)____
2. Exhibits high activity level late at night	Yes	No	(F)____	(D)____	(I)____
3. Increases goal setting	Yes	No	(F)____	(D)____	(I)____
4. Has unrealistic expectations of skills	Yes	No	(F)____	(D)____	(I)____
5. Displays rapid and insistent speech	Yes	No	(F)____	(D)____	(I)____
6. Has all-or-nothing mentality	Yes	No	(F)____	(D)____	(I)____
7. Goes on spending sprees	Yes	No	(F)____	(D)____	(I)____
8. Exhibits aggressiveness	Yes	No	(F)____	(D)____	(I)____
9. Displays touchy, irritable, "in-your-face" manner	Yes	No	(F)____	(D)____	(I)____
10. Drives recklessly	Yes	No	(F)____	(D)____	(I)____
11. Drinks and drives	Yes	No	(F)____	(D)____	(I)____
12. Has repeated car accidents	Yes	No	(F)____	(D)____	(I)____
13. Displays hypersexuality	Yes	No	(F)____	(D)____	(I)____
14. Displays provocativeness	Yes	No	(F)____	(D)____	(I)____
15. Lacks concern for harmful consequences	Yes	No	(F)____	(D)____	(I)____
16. Lies	Yes	No	(F)____	(D)____	(I)____
17. Makes up stories	Yes	No	(F)____	(D)____	(I)____
18. Sneaks out of class	Yes	No	(F)____	(D)____	(I)____
19. Sneaks out of house at night to party	Yes	No	(F)____	(D)____	(I)____
20. Has psychotic episodes:	Yes	No	(F)____	(D)____	(I)____
• delusions	Yes	No	(F)____	(D)____	(I)____
• hallucinations	Yes	No	(F)____	(D)____	(I)____
• paranoia	Yes	No	(F)____	(D)____	(I)____
• romantic delusions about teachers	Yes	No	(F)____	(D)____	(I)____

Depressive phase

1. Cries	Yes	No	(F)____	(D)____	(I)____
2. Exhibits gloominess	Yes	No	(F)____	(D)____	(I)____
3. Exhibits moodiness	Yes	No	(F)____	(D)____	(I)____
4. Is irritable (picks fights with others)	Yes	No	(F)____	(D)____	(I)____
5. Has tremendous fatigue	Yes	No	(F)____	(D)____	(I)____
6. Oversleeps	Yes	No	(F)____	(D)____	(I)____
7. Is lethargic	Yes	No	(F)____	(D)____	(I)____
8. Craves carbohydrates	Yes	No	(F)____	(D)____	(I)____
9. Is insecure	Yes	No	(F)____	(D)____	(I)____
10. Has separation anxiety	Yes	No	(F)____	(D)____	(I)____
11. Has low self-esteem	Yes	No	(F)____	(D)____	(I)____
12. Avoids school	Yes	No	(F)____	(D)____	(I)____
13. Feigns sickness to stay home from school	Yes	No	(F)____	(D)____	(I)____
14. Has constant physical complaints	Yes	No	(F)____	(D)____	(I)____
15. Self-isolates or pushes people away	Yes	No	(F)____	(D)____	(I)____
16. Has suicidal thoughts	Yes	No	(F)____	(D)____	(I)____
17. Displays ADHD symptoms:	Yes	No	(F)____	(D)____	(I)____
• inattention	Yes	No	(F)____	(D)____	(I)____
• impulsivity	Yes	No	(F)____	(D)____	(I)____

Source: Adapted from National Institute of Mental Health, 2005.

ANALYSIS OF RESULTS

When manic depression manifests itself, the world of the adolescent comes to a crashing halt. All of the gifts and talents that he or she has accumulated during childhood are swept away, leaving the adolescent in despair. The increase of reckless behaviors brings into question the whole issue of safety and risk taking. It is at this time that these students are more likely to gain both a sense of notoriety and a sense of isolation. An increase in the use of alcohol and drugs and addiction may manifest.

When the depression phase hits, the regular life of an adolescent becomes extremely overcomplicated and confusing. Many adolescents are unable to attend school or do previous activities with any type of ease or mastery. Evidence is present that many adolescents with bipolar disorder have symptoms of attention deficit hyperactivity disorder. Bipolar in adolescents is an evolving science and much needs to be discovered and studied. There are no set patterns which all adolescents follow. It is key that the individual observing the student be able to truly identify set patterns prior to introducing any type treatment plan. It is with ongoing collaboration with medical practitioners, parents, and educators that the behaviors and dysfunction can genuinely be identified and addressed fully.

Chapter Five

Prevalence: What Do the Statistics Say?

A review of the present literature demonstrates a wide variation in the frequency of occurrences of depression in children and adolescents. This variation appears to reflect differences in age, gender, and socio-demographic characteristics such as low social class, education, income, and minority group status, of the populations studied. It also suggests variation in diagnostic criteria or the absence of such criteria and inconsistencies in the use of the term *depression*. In some studies, depression is identified as a symptom, whereas in others, it is listed as a syndrome. Numerous studies focus on different diagnoses that lead to different results and conclusions. There does not seem to be a set consistency in the findings.

Recent epidemiologic surveys demonstrate that depression is one of the more common mental health disorders in the general population. When depression is identified using extreme scores on self-report scales, between 2 and 17 percent of students attending general-education school classes manifested moderate to severe levels of depressive symptomatology (Friedrich, Jacobs, & Reams, 1982). Special education populations tend to have a much higher prevalence. Between 14 and 54 percent of learning-disabled and seriously emotionally disturbed students manifested severe depressive symptomatology (Magg & Behrens, 1989).

In reporting depression, variables such as gender and age must be considered. While there is considerable research on the relationship of depression and gender, the association of age to depression is less understood, with peak incidence being reported for a wide range of ages. Adolescents in general, however, seem to experience higher rates of depression than do children. Prevalence rates of depression vary not only as a function of the age and gender but also of the population studied. Pediatric populations have been reported to demonstrate an increased association in the presence of depression.

According to epidemiological studies, about 2.5 percent of prepubertal children and up to 8.3 percent of adolescents in the United States have depression (Voelker, 2003). About five percent of children and adolescents in the general population suffer from depression at any given point in time. Children under stress, who experience loss, or have attention, learning, conduct or anxiety disorders are at a higher risk for depression. Depression also tends to run in families (American Academy of Child & Adolescent Psychiatry, 2005).

National Institute for Mental Health reports show that two percent of school-age children (6–12) suffer from major depression. Also indicated was that four percent of children post puberty (12 and older) suffered from major depression (National Institute of Mental Health, 2003).

The National Survey of Children's Health in 2005 reported that depression was found nationwide in children (3–17) at a level of 9.2 percent, with most having moderate to severe difficulty emotionally, with a concentration of behavior issues. In New Hampshire, the percentage of depression in children was 10.5 percent.

Raeburn (2003) estimates that 20 percent of American children and adolescents (or about 15 million of them) experience depression in their lives.

In 2003, five percent of children ages 4–17 were reported (by a parent) to have developed severe difficulties with emotions, concentration, behavior, or ability to get along with others (Centers for Disease Control and Prevention, 2005). The percentage of children with definite or severe emotional or behavioral difficulties differs by age and gender. The overall percentage for males is 6 percent. It is a low of five percent among ages 4-7 to a high of seven percent among ages 8–10, and the overall percentage for females is three percent. It ranges from a low of two percent at ages four to seven, to a high of five percent among ages 15–17 (CDC, 2005). Eight percent of children living below the poverty level have definite or severe depression as compared with six percent of children in the 100–199 percent of the poverty level, and five percent of children in nonpoor families (CDC, 2005).

Four percent of children in families with two parents, seven percent of children in mother-only families, and four percent in father-only families were reported to have definite emotional or behavioral difficulties. Nine percent of children not living with either were reported to have definite or severe difficulties. This group includes children with other relatives such as grandparents (CDC, 2005). Sixty-five percent of parents who reported their child had definite or severe emotional-behavioral difficulties also reported contacting a mental-health professional and/or physician and/or that the child received special education for these difficulties. Nine percent of parents reported that they wanted mental-health care for their child but could not afford to pay for it (CDC, 2005).

Approximately two-thirds of children and adolescents with major depressive disorder also have another mental disorder (Angold & Costello, 1993; Anderson & McGee, 1994). The most commonly associated disorders are dysthymia, anxiety disorder, a disruptive or antisocial disorder, or a substance abuse disorder.

Population studies show that at any one time between 10 and 15 percent of the child and adolescent population has symptoms of depression (Smucker et al., 1986). The prevalence of the completed diagnosis of major depression among all children ages 9 to 17 has been estimated at five percent (Shaffer & Craft, 1999). Estimates of one year prevalence in children range from 0.4 and 2.5 percent and in adolescents as high as 8.3 percent (Anderson & McGee, 1994, Garrison et al., 1997; Kessler, Walters, & Forthofer, 1998). For purposes of comparison, one year prevalence in adults is about 5.3 percent (Regier et al., 1993).

What do these statistics mean for the teacher and/or parent who may have to deal with this issue? Firstly, the numbers are very high: approximately 15 million school-age children are affected by depression. Is the school system adequately prepared to meet the needs of these children? The answer is probably no, as many teachers are not able to recognize the majority of symptoms. Conversely, parents themselves who observe many of the symptoms are at a loss until identification or labeling is done. Many believe that they simply have a very difficult or moody child.

The identification of depressed children and adolescents is hampered by limited self-referral evidence in school populations (Reynolds & Coats, 1986). There is also a tendency for some parents to deny or reject the information that their child may be suffering from an affective disorder. To some extent, the symptoms of depression, many of which are internalizing such as cognitive and somatic features, limit the identification of depressed children and adolescents by parents and teachers (Reynolds & Coats, 1986). Thus, the direct assessment of thc child may provide the best procedure for the initial identification of potentially depressed children. The school, therefore, provides an optimal setting for early identification of depressed children and adolescents.

Assessment is basic to the identification and study of depression and is a means for determining the effective treatment. Further, the expression of depression (or at least our ability to identify depression) appears to increase from childhood to adolescence. There is variance among identified populations studied, with the lowest frequency found among the general population and the highest found among psychiatric patient populations. The rates appear to be higher among several at-risk populations of children.

There are too few relevant studies by which to draw any conclusion about rising depression rates during adolescence in females compared to males. No single biological, psychological, or social factor is likely to account entirely for the switch. A longitudinal study is needed in which depression and a number of biological factors, such as hormonal changes and pubertal development, are investigated. Along with these biological factors, psychological factors, such as self-concept and personal goals, and social factors, such as restrictions on freedom and choice, expectations of others, life events, and victimization are assessed periodically in a large group of males and females from age 10 to at least early adulthood. Only with such a study can the contribution of these factors to differences in depression be adequately assessed.

Better assessment tools will lead to more accurate reporting of the prevalence of depression and possibly a more accurate reflection of the true numbers of depressed children and adolescents.

Chapter Six

Assessments: How Is Depression Measured and Reported?

This chapter will focus on discussing the different types of assessment inventories and tests used in the diagnosis of depression. The presentation of instruments herein does not constitute endorsement of it. It is hoped that by introducing these instruments, teachers and parents will be better informed about the test results and options available when trying to obtain a diagnosis or an understanding of the details often found in depression and depressive symptoms.

According to the National Mental Health Association (NMHA), October 9 is National Depression Screening Day, a nationwide program designed to provide information about the signs, symptoms, and treatment of depression, bipolar disorder, and other mental-health disorders (U.S. Dept. of Health and Human Services, 1999). The program's mandate is to build public awareness and education on the topic of depression. Its function is to demystify depression and make it a household word so that individuals will request at early stages and access mental-health services and will not wait until the depression has advanced to perilous levels.

Measure of Self-Esteem (Rosenberg)

This test was developed to measure adolescents' feelings of self-worth or self-acceptance. It includes 10 items that are scored using a four-point response from the individual ranging from strongly disagree to strongly agree (Adler, 1998).

Reynolds Depression-Screening Inventory

The purpose is to screen for symptoms of depression for the age group between 18–89 years. This inventory is produced in a booklet containing 19 items that measure severity of depressive symptoms. This test requires a fifth-grade reading level. The test takes 5–15 minutes and can be taken in groups or as a self-report for individuals. The booklet is provided with a professional manual which describes the development, administration, and scoring (Reynolds & Kobak, 1996).

Personality Inventory for Children (Marilyn T. Erickson, 1982)

The development of assessments and screening in children is difficult because researchers rely mostly on parents, teachers, and counselors. Assessments are a tool but further investigations into their external environment are crucial.

The personality inventory developed by Wirt, Lachar, Klinedinst, and Seat (1983) is a test administered to parents of children who are suspected to have depression. The booklet consists of 600 items to be completed by the parents or another individual, such as a counselor or teacher. The test respondent is asked to indicate if the statement is true of the individual. The Personality Inventory for Children can be scored and interpreted by computer via Western Psychological Service Test Report prepaid mail, in answer sheets, microcomputer disk, or fax service.

Scale for Assessing Emotional Disturbance

The Scale for Assessing Emotional Disturbance (SAED) is designed to assist in identifying students who may be experiencing emotional and/or behavioral difficulties within the educational setting. It is also reported to be useful as a screening device, as it is a tool for research and a method by which to measure a student's progress. The scale comprises 52 items that encompass seven subscales and a single item that highlights overall educational performance. These seven subscales include inability to learn, e.g., "Homework skills are poor" (eight items); relationship problems, e.g., "Has few or no friends" (six items); inappropriate behavior, e.g. "Cruel to peers" (10 items); unhappiness or depression, e.g., "Lacks self-confidence" (seven items); physical symptoms or fears, e.g., "Anxious, Worried, Tense" (eight items); socially maladjusted, e.g., "Runs away from home" (six items); and overall competence (seven items). The single item highlighting overall academic performance is termed *adversely affects educational performance*.

The actual rating form is broken down into three domains that include a) student competence characteristics, b) student emotional and behavioral problems, and c) adversely affect educational performance. A psychologist, teacher, parent, caregiver, or any other individual knowledgeable about the individual and his or her behaviors may complete the SAED. Professionals who have appropriate knowledge and background about the SAED specifically and psychometric properties and psychological interpretation in general should complete scoring. Respondents to the SAED are asked to rate the child on each statement using a Likert-type scale. Items within the domain of Student Emotional and Behavioral Problems are scored on a four-point scale, while the Student Competence Characteristics are on a five-point scale and the Adversely Affects Educational Performance is on a six-point scale. There are also eight open-ended questions at the conclusion of the scale that offer ratings related to the student's athletic, academic, social, family, and community strengths (Dumont & Rauch, 2000).

Children's Depression Inventory

This inventory is the most widely used self-report of childhood depression. It is an extension of the Beck Depression Inventory. The Children's Depression Inventory (CDI) contains 27 items with three statements about the particular depressive symptom. For each item, the individual is asked to select the statement that best describes his or her feelings for the past two weeks. The first statement reflects minimal depressive symptoms with no severity (scoring 0). The second statement is moderate symptoms scoring 1, and the last statement is more severe with a score of 2. The total scores range from 0–54. The time frame for reporting is two weeks prior to the test. Psychologists rate this easiest self-report depression measure. Concurrent validity of the CDI is supported by high positive correlations with self-reported anxiety and negative correlations with self-esteem. The CDI test is administered to individuals between 6–17 years of age. It is used for clinicians and counselors to assess a child's loss of interest and self-worthlessness, and supports diagnosis and treatment planning. Although the CDI is a reliable measure of current distress, it cannot be used alone to measure a diagnostic depressive disorder (Hersen & Ollendick, 1993).

Beck Depression Inventory

This scale is one of the most commonly used to diagnose depression in adolescents and adults. It is comprised of 21 depressive symptoms in a multiple-choice format, and uses a four-point scale that reflects a hierarchical increase of intensity. Each item consists of four statements describing varying degrees of severity of a depressive symptom. The respondent chooses which statement is most accurate. Total scores range from 0–63. Scores over 16 are considered moderate to more severe depression (Hersen & Ollendick, 1993). The BDI is used as a screening instrument and as a measure of the severity of adolescent depression. The validity of this test is high and most accurate with adolescents (Hersen & Ollendick, 1993). There was a relationship between the patient's BDI scores and the patient's clinical state (Beck, 1967).

Reynolds Adolescent Depression Scale

This scale is used by thousands of clinicians and school personnel to screen for depressive symptoms in adolescents. This is a 30-item self-report with four basic dimensions to evaluate depressive symptomatology: dysphonic mood, anhedonia/negative affect, negative self-evaluation, and somatic complaints. It includes 30 items that are rated on a four-point scale. Total score represents normal, mild, moderate, to severe depression (Psychological Publications, Inc., 2004).

Children's Depression Scale

This is a 66-item scale with 48 depressive and 18 positive items that yield two separate scores (Hersen & Ollendick, 1993). The depressive scale has five subscales: affective responses, social problems, self-esteem, preoccupation with sickness or death, and guilt. This test has strong consistency in differentiating between depressed and non-depressed individuals (Hersen & Ollendick, 1993).

This is but a small representation of the types of tests that may be used by professionals in identifying the possibilities of depression. They can also be utilized as an effective screening tool. The information gathered can then be investigated, and a recommendation may be made for further evaluation. Under no circumstances should the results of one inventory or test be used to diagnose depression in children.

Depression is multifaceted and the presentation of its many symptoms can be manifested in multiple ways. This is why the identification and later diagnosis must come from a variety of perspectives. This is the only true way to truly ascertain that depression is present in the child or adolescent. Rushing diagnosis without proper evidence can obviously do more harm then good. Giving a child medication that he or she does not need can create significant health and illness issues. The most effective way to identify depression is through multiple sources with very clear evidence based in fact, not emotion or simply observation. There must be clinical proof. There must be evidence substantiated with excellent data, testing, and interviews. An excellent evaluation leads to a more effective intervention, which in turn leads to better overall treatment.

Chapter Seven

What Is Influencing Youth Today?

Life in the new millennium has been a challenge for many. How does a teacher or a parent know what to do when a child or student expresses feelings of depression, anxiety, peer pressure, or low self-esteem? For many, there are no easy solutions to these problems. At times, the responses are based solely on instinct or experience. The decisions made for follow-up or lack of follow-through are inconsistent and/or unreliable, as they are based upon insufficient information.

At the first signs of disturbance, it is necessary to ascertain what is anxiety-based and what is depression-based. Anxiety is defined herein as a feeling associated with some fear or dread of a negatively anticipated outcome to a situation or event. Anxiety can be manifested in a series of ways: phobia, generalized anxiety disorder, school refusal, oppositional defiance, stress, and/or obsessive-compulsive disorder. Depression is defined as a feeling associated with loss. The loss can be tangible or psychological. Depression may also include feelings of anger, helplessness, hopelessness, a lack of forgiveness, and/or trauma. Depression can be manifested in bad mood, and mild depressive feelings. It may be situational and/or reactive, and may be chronic, where the depression is a whole-body illness. Eating, sleeping, and daily functioning and coping are often severely affected.

Once the distinction has been made between anxiety and depression, parents or teachers can begin to understand the differences, symptoms, and signs to observe or anticipate. The following disturbances may be observed: missed school or poor school performance; changes in eating and/or sleeping habits; withdrawal from friends and/or activities once enjoyed; persistent sadness and hopelessness; overreaction to anger, criticism, rage, or problems with authority; indecision, lack of concentration, or forgetfulness; poor self-esteem or guilt; frequent physical complaints, such as headaches and stomachaches; lack of enthusiasm, low energy or motivation; drug and/or alcohol abuse; and thoughts of death or suicide or suicidal behavior.

There are four key factors influencing children today: (1) biology, (2) psychology, (3) society, and (4) family. Each of these factors will be discussed individually.

BIOLOGICAL FACTORS

The first influence is biology. Within this domain are three areas that will be explored: genetics, prenatal care, and environmental toxins. For many decades, supporting evidence has linked depression as inherited from one or both parents. The evidence gathered is often linked to immediate relative exposure. If a parent, grandparent, or aunts and uncles have had or still have clinical depression, the chances are 70 percent that one of the children will inherit this gene. For many generations this link was not made and, often, families floundered as individuals suffered symptoms and mental breakdowns. It appeared to be prevalent in families and it was only through research that the links were found. When psychologists and/or psychiatrists evaluate for depression, a family history is taken to determine if there is a genetic link as an explanation for the symptoms being manifested. Much of the research on children and adolescents with depression has been conducted with those who attend mental-health clinics and with patients who tend to have the more severe and recurrent forms of depression. With this limitation, research has shown that between 20 and 50 percent of depressed children and adolescents have a family history of depression (Kovacs, 1996). Family research has found that children of depressed parents are more than three times as likely as children with non-depressed parents to experience a depressive disorder (Birmaher et al., 1996). It is not clear whether the relationship between parent and childhood depression is derived from genetic factors, or whether depressed parents create an environment that increases the likelihood of a mental disorder developing in their children.

Depression is an acutely distressing, debilitating, and at times life-threatening illness. It is also a recurring disease. The genetic link is in the area of brain chemistry. People who are depressed may have diminished amounts of the neurotransmitter serotonin available to activate brain cells. One cell releases serotonin and the latter travels across the synapse and activates the second cell. The message-sending cell also re-absorbs some serotonin, making it unavailable to the receiving cell, so the receiving cell does not get enough serotonin, thus creating an imbalance in the thinking processes (which seems to be an inherited deficiency). As this is not a visible disability, it is often very hard to pinpoint whether the depression is chemically based, situational, or environmentally based. Usually, once medication has been prescribed, there is an obvious improvement in functioning and coping on the part of the child. It has been documented that children as early as five or six years of age have manifested depression because of the inherited gene.

Some of the core symptoms of depression, such as changes in appetite and sleep patterns, are related to the function of hypothalamus. The hypothalamus is, in turn, closely tied to the function of the pituitary gland. Abnormalities of pituitary function, such as increased rates of circulating cortisol and hypo- or hyperthyroidism, are well-established features of depression in adults. In some families, major depression also seems to occur in successive generations. However, it can also occur in people who have no family history of depression. Whether inherited or not, major depressive disorder is often associated with changes in brain structures or brain function.

Gestational time within the womb is the time in our development when all the systems are programmed to happen in a certain order and at a specific rate. When there is an interruption of this routine or plan, problems begin to manifest themselves in a variety of issues later on in a child's life. However, what happens in the uterus is not readily obvious until incidents or stressors in the child's life create a scenario wherein the child is unable to perform or function in his or her environment. A woman who is unaware of good prenatal health may unintentionally cause damage to one or more stages of development of her unborn child. Research exists about the use of alcohol, nicotine, drugs, and their impact on the developing fetus. It seems that the fragility of the developing child and all the different compositions and organizations of the mental and physical network create many opportunities for necessary factors to be left out or not given the chance to develop appropriately. Lack of proper nutrition, health care, and guidance may deprive a fetus of receiving the proper balance of nutrients on which it depends to develop appropriately. There is a direct correlation between excellent prenatal care and well-functioning babies. Direct educational practices and interventions given to expectant mothers have a direct effect on producing fewer depressed children because of genetic or prenatal neglect.

Because of the rapid growth in industry and the misuse of the environment's resources, new toxins exist in water, food, and air. The emergence of these toxins has led to an increase in illnesses, allergies, and disabilities. Since the 1960s there has been a steady increase in toxins found in human DNA, which in turn directly affects unborn fetuses during development. How can a foreign agent not affect the developing fetus? Each year, as new levels of toxins are found in some communities, there is a resultant increase in numbers of child cancers, asthma, and depression. These toxins are proficient at melding into the genetic makeup of an individual. Toxins lay dormant, waiting to be passed on to the next generation at the moment of conception. This creates another level of impairment in one form or another, as the child inherits depression or cancer and is destined to be plagued by it.

PSYCHOLOGICAL FACTORS

The second influence is psychology. Several areas will be addressed: temperament, personality, intelligence, cognitive activity, behavior, mood-affect, and self-esteem.

Temperament is a curiously interesting characteristic of human beings. Why are some children easy going and relaxed, while others are hyperactive, impulsive, easily frustrated, reactive, and depressive? It is believed but not well supported by many research studies that temperament is defined and developed within the womb and is influenced by the type of pregnancy the woman is experiencing. If the woman is enjoying a calm pregnancy, this calmness is transferred to her unborn child. If the opposite is true, that negative energy and hormonal factors are transferred to the unborn fetus. This child tends to be much more needy and demanding.

Acting out appears to be a link to possible development of depression. May one generalize and claim that this is always the case? Of course not. However, an informal survey on the part of the author indicated that children born of difficult pregnancies tended to exhibit behavioral problems.

Personality is as unique as the individual. Even identical twins are different, although they have the same genetic makeup. Personality appears to play a major role in coping with life situations and circumstances. Some personalities are more prone to depression because of the level of intensity and/or involvement with their emotional sides. Right-brain individuals tend to over-personalize events and are often unable to see the possibility of solutions and/or resolution to their emotional chaos. Left-brain individuals are more likely to adapt to overanalyze the issues and are unable to get closure or a sense of control that would allow them to take charge. There are many personality assessment inventories available by which to discuss the role of personality and responses to situations or stimuli.

Understanding the temperament and/or personality of a child is key to learning whether or not they are at risk of becoming depressed because of personality influences. The first type, "troubleshooters," are children who are exciting, optimistic, desire freedom, hunger for action, impulsive, and independent. They pride themselves on fearlessness, boldness, and cleverness. They tend to ignore rules of such organizations as schools, preschools, sports clubs, etc. Troubleshooters are risk takers and need support from others. They find it very difficult to be told how to work and/or to follow standard procedures. It is predictable that this personality temperament may become depressed.

These children will rebel from rules and expectations, especially those of which they have not helped construct. They want to believe they have an impact on or influence in their environment. They want to be in control of their destiny and choose what they think is best, and are especially anxious not to have an adult do it for them or take away that choice. Failure to be recognized leads to more unreasonable expectations that these children will put upon themselves. They will want to prove their worthiness and value, and may go to extremes to do so. The behaviors of manipulation, lying, and magnification of situations will manifest once these children have the belief that no matter what they do it never will be good enough. The beliefs and irrational thinking patterns may replace the strengths these children possess, hence the strengths are no longer available to help these children out of the pit that they may have created. The need to be free and independent is a driving force in their personality makeup. If life circumstances dictate that a time of confinement or dependency becomes necessary, these children will begin to act out physically or emotionally. As previously stated, depression can be both internal and external. These children are more likely to be external with severe acting-out behaviors leading to violence and aggression toward the people they believe are blocking their access to freedom or independence.

The fact that troubleshooters respond quickly to the ideas of others and are amenable most of the time may assist in reaching them if they should begin the decline into situational depression. They can change their position as new facts and ideas arise. The formula for redirecting these students is to help them see new ways not as something to be repelled but a way in which they can enhance their already existing skills and strengths. By presenting new ideas so that they have some input and control will lead to better engagement and devotion to the new idea or plan. Helping troubleshooters to be contributors will help them to feel more committed and collaborative in nature toward others.

The second type of temperament is the "harmonizer." These children work to create harmony in their lives. They like compliments such as how accurate and thorough they are. They pride themselves on being responsible, loyal, and industrious. They crave an abundance of appreciation. They can be insensitive to authority in a school setting. They focus on procedures rather than people. Harmonizers are easily influenced by other people whom they perceive as more powerful than themselves. Stress and possible depression may be triggered when people in their lives do not follow standard procedures or rules. If deadlines are not met, it may send them spiraling. Once they begin the descent, they become impatient and want others to get to the point and stick to it. A child who has teachers or parents who are spontaneous would complicate this child's life and may trigger depressive-like symptoms. Harmonizers may speak on weaknesses in themselves and others rather than strengths. They hyper-focus on what is wrong and what is not going well. Harmonizers withhold compliments as a way of controlling others to do what they want. At times they are very straightforward, confrontational, and lacking in tact. The solution is to provide this child with stability. It is within this stability that this child finds his or her comfort and energy. Chaos will lead a child to feel helpless and hopelessness. It is best to keep the child focused on what it is that they can and cannot control. Secondly, it is important to stop them from hyper-focusing on what is not working and focus on what is. They can remain functional provided that the adults in their lives are good role models and give great examples of what to do when problems do occur. Problem solving and attention to detail are strengths for these children, and they need to be maximized to their full potential.

The third type of personality temperament is the "analyst." Analysts strive to do things well under varying circumstances and are the most self-critical of all the personalities. They always are trying to improve by continuously monitoring their progress, and checking their skills. They are their own worst critics. They must understand all components of a situation in all aspects, and settle for nothing less than the best for themselves as well as others. As a result, they are perfectionists who become tense and compulsive in their behavior when they are under too much stress. Thus, depression looms.

Analysts are quick to question and are often very forward-thinking, problem solvers, precise, persistent, and, at times, very open-minded. They become depressed or dysfunctional when asked to do something unreasonable. Traditions or personal bias get in the way. One way to help these children is for them to become more self-aware by reflecting on their actions and thoughts. Analysts sometimes make those around them feel intellectually inadequate, defensive, withdrawn, and less likely to share their ideas. When they do not get their way, they resort to all the behaviors listed previously. Analysts listen closely to new ideas and can accept change easily as long as it makes sense. Reviewing all the components of the idea in a systematic way with the child is more apt to get compliance. Lack of understanding and comprehension on the part of the child will only lead to resistance and frustration. Depending upon the level of dysfunction in the child, sabotaging behaviors may become apparent in order for him or her to regain a sense of control. A positive trait of these children is that once they have mastered a new skill, they move on to something else.

The fourth kind of personality temperament is the "seeker." Seekers constantly look for an identity that is uniquely their own. These children do not want to be lost in a crowd, they want to be above the crowd. Their primary motivation is the need to make a difference and to maintain individuality. Making a difference in their world can satisfy the need for a unique identity. They experience life as a drama, each encounter being more important than the previous one. They are known for having a strong desire to accomplish goals, but they tend to go between many ideas without completion. This behavior pattern creates much stress for them as well as the people in their lives. This inability to be boxed in makes seekers great candidates for issues at school, especially in classroom routines or courses they perceive as too restrictive. They will rebel for the sake of their principles. Seekers want to be given choice, and when they believe that choice is taken away or the choices given are unacceptable, helplessness and hopelessness leading to situational or reactive depression may appear. They enjoy bringing out the best in others, and speak often and enthusiastically on the potential of others, and of themselves. They are not interested in things, but in people. They seek relationships because they must interact with others. Once this motivation is recognized and allowed to develop, they will be free of any type of depressive-like symptoms. Seekers have excellent problem-solving skills, and need to have the opportunity to use their best assets of caring, sharing, and relating.

Children with higher intelligence seem to be at greater risk for depression. They have difficulty in problem solving or recognizing their own limited thinking. They ruminate about issues that could be resolved if they were able to see beyond the obvious factors. They become predictable in their responses. They lose the ability to analyze and identify what the problem is, look at alternatives, choose one, do it, and then re-evaluate the results. Their higher intelligence usually gives them the skills to analyze and solve; however, in these situations they seem to lose this skill and become highly emotional, depressive, and suicidal.

Children of lower intelligence appear to demonstrate their depression at a more primal level. It is demonstrated in specific acting-out behaviors that are easily identifiable and addressed. They tend to be more open to solutions, and in need of guidance from the adults in their lives. The highly intelligent children tend to isolate themselves when depressed as they have the belief that they should be able to solve the issues or problems on their own, while the less intelligent child will look to the adult for the added support and care. The latter child is often easier to work with as he or she does not have the same level of cognition as the adults with whom he or she is working. The gifted child, however, often surpasses the adults in his or her world and does not see them as equals or supports to help him or her solve problems. In fact, thoughts of superiority often prevent gifted children from solving the problem or using others in a collaborative way as support. They often feel that they are isolated and doomed to failure. These thoughts then lead to major depressive symptoms that could possibly have been avoided if support and treatment would have been accepted earlier. These students may resort to alcohol and drugs and will develop addictions to mask their depression, while the less gifted children will often respond well to treatment and intervention.

Cognitive factors are often unrecognized as major contributors to depression in children. For more than two decades there has been considerable interest in the relationship between a particular mind-set or approach to perceiving external events, and a predisposition to depression. The mind-set in question is known as a pessimistic attribution bias that was proposed by Aaron Beck in 1987. A child with this mind-set readily assumes personal blame for negative events. For example, a child may attribute family turmoil to be his or her fault. The child believes that everything he or she does is wrong, which is part of a mind-set that relates that one negative experience is part of a pattern of many other negative events. This child also thinks that a currently negative situation will endure permanently. For example, the child may be thinking, "Nothing I do is going to make anything better." Pessimistic children and adolescents will often take a characteristically negative view of positive events. They believe that positive events are a result of someone else's effort, and that they are isolated events unlikely to recur. Children with this mind-set have a tendency to react more passively, and are generally more helpless and respond more ineffectively to negative events than the general population.

There is uncertainty in the field over whether this mind-set precedes depression or is a manifestation of prior depressive episodes that perhaps went unnoticed. There is evidence that children and adolescents who previously have been depressed may learn, during their depression, to interpret events in a pessimistic way. This mind-set provides a rich environment in which the child reacts similarly to negative events experienced after recovery. Thus, it could be one of the reasons why previously depressed children and adolescents are frequently at risk for a continued or recurring depression.

Perceptions of hopelessness, negative views about one's own competence, poor self-esteem, and a sense of responsibility for negative events may all be contributing factors to the possibility that the child or adolescent will contemplate or attempt suicide. It is difficult for a child to feel adequate if he or she is not succeeding in school. A child's educational success measures his or her ability to succeed outside of the family. Parental satisfaction with a child also can vary with the child's grades. Language and learning disabilities, attention deficit hyperactivity disorder, school phobia, and any other condition that interferes with a child's learning therefore easily can increase the risk for depression. Likewise, a depressed child's response to treatment may be measured in part by increased academic success.

Adverse experiences such as parental death or separation during childhood and adolescence raise the risk for depression in adulthood. It appears that the effects of this loss may be mediated by psychosocial factors before or after the event. Numerous studies indicate that there is a direct link to depression if there is significantly more negative life events, especially in the domain of school, relationship with friends or parents, health, or romantic relationships up to 12 months before the onset of depression. This indicates that the child and/or adolescent may be ruminating about these situations for a year before the manifestations come to light. Studies of depressed adults recalling their early family relationships, children of depressed parents, and depressed youth have shown that their family interactions are characterized by more conflict, child maltreatment, rejection, and problems with communication, and less expression of affect and support, compared with families without depression present. Depressed parents often experience difficulties in the parenting that may reflect the symptoms of their own disorders. Conversely, parenting role problems may be secondary to interaction with a depressed, irritable, or oppositional child. One must also be aware that parenting difficulties may be due to alcoholism, personality disorders, and/or other psychopathology. The stress caused by these specific issues may have more impact on parenting than parental depression. Several studies suggest that parenting difficulties may not be specific to depressed parents but common to parents who are distressed because of family, marital, economic, medical, and psychological problems. There is an increased risk of any psychiatric disorder in children when parents have poor functioning or conflicted relationships with their children.

Parents with untreated depression may affect a child's development of social, emotional, cognitive, and interpersonal skills, as well as the type of or absence of a bond or emotional connection between child and parent. Children and adolescents with depression are at high risk for suicidal behavior, substance abuse (including nicotine dependence), physical illness, early pregnancy, exposure to negative life events, and poor work, academic and psychosocial functioning. An excellent gauge for the likeliness of depression is directly related to the level of self-esteem a child possesses. The higher the child's beliefs of self-worth, self-competence, self-control, and self-reliance, the less likely that the child or adolescent will suffer or experience depression.

Depressed children with low self-esteem will manifest some of the following maladaptive behaviors: withdrawn, shy, unhappy, negative feelings, and thoughts about self are revealed physically (slouching posture, averted eyes), verbally (negative or critical remarks about self), academically (lack of effort, little interest or pride in work), and socially (reluctant to interact with classmates); withdrawn, uncommunicative: seldom initiates associations with other children or the teacher; when spoken to, responds inaudibly or tersely, or fails to reply; aloof: approaches by teacher are met with a nonchalant, "who cares" attitude; self-deprecating remarks: negative or critical comments about self expressed orally or in writing; could be about appearance, social ability, academic ability, or self-worth; helpless/hopeless: expressions of inability to cope with situations or problems, particularly in stressful conditions and/or pessimism about the future; sad, unhappy: chronic sad demeanor, with possible incidents of tearfulness, frequent outbursts of tears; attention seeking: frequently demands attention from teacher or parent through fawning behavior.

Students with poor self-esteem manifested in depression show an increase in poor hygiene, including consistently dirty hair and bodies. There is obvious tiredness, as the child appears fatigued even in the early morning. Certain habits and mannerisms manifest such as nail biting, sniffling, nose picking, talking to self and frequent absences from school for a variety of vague physical complaints. Academic underachievement becomes more prominent. Anxiety becomes more pronounced with an expressed or apparent fear of school-related activities such as tests, assignments, and new work. An increase in lack of attentiveness where there is lack of attention to lessons as they are being taught. Assigned work for class or home is incomplete. Distractibility and inattentiveness to class work because of daydreaming, wandering about the class, watching or bothering classmates, playing, or fidgeting all become ways of escaping from the feelings of inadequacy and low self-esteem.

Students with low self-esteem also have social-adjustment issues that may lead to depression. They have insecurity in peer relationships, and few, if any, friends in class. They seek self-isolation, finding places and activities away from other children, and teachers and parents. They exhibit submissiveness with peers because of feelings of inferiority. They tend to have negative peer relationships and are disliked and ostracized by classmates because of unfriendliness and/or poor social skills. Because of the fact that they do want to be included, there may be an increase in acting out, clowning behavior, and/or temper outbursts.

The depressive child is caught in a vicious circle. Distressed feelings lead to maladaptive behaviors that result in experiences that reinforce the distressed feelings. There is, unfortunately, no magic solution. However, improvement may be achieved by modifying the maladaptive behaviors. Each new and more constructive behavior the child learns results in experiences that ultimately disconfirm the negative feelings about self and replace them with more positive feelings and actions. With hope, this leads to a child better able to cope with his or her depression.

SOCIETAL FACTORS

The third influence on children and adolescents is societal. Within this area the following will be discussed: school, friends, Internet, extracurricular activities, community, and church/religion.

School is the place where children spend most of their early childhood and adolescent years. It is their job. They are sent to school to be socialized, educated, and informed on becoming contributing citizens. They are expected to be respectful, kind, and responsible. They come to school to learn and grow, especially to learn skills that will empower them to become productive members of society. School is great for many children and adolescents who fly through the system and are very successful. However, other children are not. They learn very quickly that they are not proficient at their job. They experience failure at an early age. They get all the life and motivation taken out of them by educators who do not recognize their learning styles or learning disabilities. The children begin to fail repeatedly in their academic work, thus creating more adversarial relationships with parents and teachers. Eventually, the children give up and fall prey to situational depression, which if unaddressed may grow into chronic depression.

Educators who have a good pulse of their classrooms are usually the first to recognize a child's descent into depression. They see the downfall, address it in a proactive way with modifications, with extra time spent in instruction, and teach the child in a way that he or she can be successful. The child or adolescent is given work that he or she can master. Through the proper channels, instructional materials and content are presented in a way that the child can understand. A sense of mastery will lead to increased self-esteem, and a possible increase in motivation and output.

Children who do well in school are less likely to suffer situational depression. If they earn good grades, are recognized for their efforts, and made to feel that they are making contributions, such children are more likely to be depression-free.

Numerous studies indicate that when children feel connected, capable, and contributing to their school life, they are more likely to be involved and active members of the school community. Failure on the part of the school to create this kind of climate leads to children who are apathetic, and who have no sense of connectedness and/or pride in their participation in that particular environment.

Do schools create depressed children? Absolutely! Overcrowded, impersonal schools where each student and faculty member is but a number only fosters depression. Rules and expectations must exist to maintain order. However, do many schools require and/or demand sameness for inclusion? Absolutely! If students are too different from the norm, they are either isolated or shunned by peers or faculty. A prime example is that many of our schools are divided by groups. Some students are "cool," others are "jocks," others are "geeks and nerds," and the last group is often the "misfits" who do not fit anywhere, not even with one another. Children in the last group are the most at risk for depression. They have no way of being connected or sharing a group identity. They are on their own. Their differences will result in teasing or taunting from their peers. Bullying is present in the schools. Zero-tolerance policies exist to prevent violence, however, it rarely catches the daily episodes of covert harassment.

The fatal shooting at Columbine High School in Colorado is an example of the system being unable to recognize the potential for disaster when students are persecuted by their peers on a daily basis. In this situation, students acted out their depression in a rage and killing spree that left many people dead and a nation in crisis.

Students who do not act out publicly manifest their depression in school in other ways. They may become the drug- or alcohol-addicted, truant, and/or oppositional students. There is an increase in eating disorders and self-injurious behaviors (such as cutting, phobias) that seem to be a direct result of that particular child's school life or experience. Children do not become alcoholics, addicts, prostitutes, or anorexic because they feel good about themselves. Somewhere along the way, school, family, and/or society have failed to protect them. Children resort to criminal activity because they see no alternatives. Schools play a role in helping children become successful, but they also need to offer support services for children who are not coping. It is a school's responsibility to meet the needs of its charges. If depression begins to manifest itself, the school needs to have the resources and skills by which to mobilize to provide the child with the best services and support available.

Friends and friendships are primary to all human beings. We are social beings who need to feel accepted and have a sense of belonging. This need is often cited as a primary source for child and adolescent depression. The lack of a friendship network will lead to a sense of isolation and rejection. Children want to play with others and to feel that someone cares about them. Adolescents want to be part of a group that values and accepts them. There seems to be a direct relationship between onset of depression and the entrance to adolescence and middle school. Children who were once friends in elementary school no longer commingle in middle school. The quirky behaviors in elementary school were tolerated, but once in middle school, these behaviors spawn ridicule and isolation. Children who have always felt included soon become outsiders. They no longer have a support system. Their friends have abandoned them for "cooler" kids. Depression looms in this scenario.

There is an increase in female depression at the onset of middle school. Girls tend to be more socially oriented, more dependent on social relationships, and more vulnerable to losses of social relationships than boys. This increases their vulnerability to the interpersonal stresses common in teenagers. There is also evidence to suggest that the methods girls use to cope with stress may entail less denial and more focused and repetitive thinking. The higher prevalence of teenage girls being depressed could be a result of greater vulnerability, combined with coping mechanisms different than those of boys. It seems to be more important to females to be accepted at middle schools and high schools than it is for boys. Boys have a tendency to move more freely through the system, though they too have many hurdles and expectations. They may not personalize the situations, or are just better at ignoring and internalizing the anger (which may lead to future acting-out behaviors at a later time).

Adolescent boys mask their depression with alcohol or drugs, or by the socially acceptable habit of working excessively long hours. Depression typically shows up in these adolescents not as feelings of hopelessness or helplessness, but irritability, anger, and discouragement. Hence, depression may be difficult to recognize in boys. Even if a boy realizes his depression, he may be less willing than the girls are to seek help. Encouragement and support from family members can make a difference.

A child who once played often with friends may prefer to be alone and without interests. People and events that were once fun now bring little joy to the depressed child. If the child begins to isolate from his or her friends, he or she is at an increased risk for suicide, alcohol abuse, or other drug abuse as a way to feel better. Children who act out at home and school may also be suffering from depression. It is at this time that adult observation is key to identifying whether this child is connected to friends. Lack of friendships is a telling signal.

The Internet is the next factor that has changed our lives in the late 20th century and into the 21st. It has revolutionized how we communicate. It has become a source of information without end. It provides children with answers to any questions. In the past, children needed to ask their parents or teachers for the information. Today they go online and find it faster than turning pages in a book. The Internet has also created a generation of students who have little physical contact with other human beings. So much is now done online and without need for human interaction, except through an instant messenger service or a text message. Children and adolescents have begun to interact socially on the Internet. Many of them become victims of predators who lure them through a variety of means and promises. If a child has a predisposition toward depression and/or is experiencing one at the moment, predators capitalize on this information and are then able to use the child for their own deviant purposes.

Instant messaging has become the premiere form of communication for adolescents and their friends. They use it at school, at home, and on their cell phones. While facilitating instant communication, online activity may also destroy an adolescent's whole world as it exists. A rumor sent over the Internet to hundreds of students can destroy an individual's world. The Internet may be used to manipulate and destroy other adolescents who may be a barrier to the accomplishment of a certain goal on the part of a particular group. There have been situations nationwide of students committing suicide because of what had been said or spread over the Internet. Adult supervision and monitoring are keys to the prevention of Internet-related violence.

Extracurricular activities have been known to prevent some of the more reactional of depressions. Participation in clubs, sports, and other organizations fuels the need to belong and, thus, creates a sense of acceptance and value. Students who participate in sports in any capacity are less likely to experience depression. A shared interest builds collegiality and support. If students happen to become depressed, they are more likely to reach out to their colleagues for support. If they receive support and understanding, they are more likely to problem solve. The mentality of many teams is to work together, be there for one another not unlike a family. Students who feel disconnected from their peers are more likely to feel alone and rejected. Sports teams and various clubs provide an outlet that serves a dual function, one of belonging, and the other of support. Placing a depressed child on a team or club, however, will not cure his or her depression. Prior membership in one of these organizations may lessen the degree of depression.

The community in which a child lives is also a factor in the possibility of depressive occurrence. Children who live in economically distressed areas are more likely to experience poverty, crime, and issues of personal safety, and are at a greater risk of depression. Poverty leads to despair, a lack of basic necessities, usually more parental strife, and possibly constant displacement or homelessness, which leads to children becoming more apt to experience depression because of the lack of control they may have in their young lives. For some children, depression is triggered by a lack of proper nutrition. Once that is regulated, depression may retreat or lessen.

The influence of crime and personal safety for children is paramount in whether they will develop fears about their daily existence. If they walk to school in fear of being killed, children develop feelings of helplessness and hopelessness. For some, post-traumatic stress disorder sets in with depression and leads to a multitude of problems. A child's perception about safety will either foster or negate a depression from taking hold. Safer streets and schools equal fewer depressed and frightened individuals.

Adherence to an organized religion may be a major support for some and, for others, a source of depression. Religion can influence its followers to seeking the support they need in their spirituality. For others, the lack of guidance or answers to questions or events lead them to feel abandoned by their church. In the case of an accident, one may question why God "allowed" it to happen. Having no answer may lead to a questioning of one's faith, and, thus, feelings of hopelessness in controlling one's destiny. Children and adolescents look toward their parents as role models and guides. It is with this guidance that many are able to overcome issues that create chaos in their lives. However, one cannot take solace in something one cannot see or feel.

Organized religions have as their mandates a propensity to guide, support, and attempt to "save" their faithful from eternal damnation. In some cases, the organized group has caused the depression for the child and adolescent because the individual is not following doctrine or doing as he or she is told. The individual is challenging the status quo. Many adolescents become depressed because they are not able to follow all the rules and, instead of disappointing and/or bringing shame upon their names or families, they choose to suffer in silence. Some adolescents run away, act out, or commit suicide as their only option to escaping the chains of their beliefs and upbringing.

Organized religions do not of course, set out to create depression in children and adolescents. However, they create environments with rules and expectations that may in turn lead to the possibility that some of their members will develop depression when there is a perception of not being able to fit in or be successful within the existing parameters as set out by the leaders of that religion.

FAMILY FACTORS

The dynamics of the family unit are paramount to successful treatment and intervention of a depressed child. The physical makeup of the family also has a considerable impact on how well the child or adolescent feels supported during the depression. At times, the issues within the family are the root cause of depression, especially when situational depression is present.

An intact family unit, if functional, can be a great support for a child. If the family is intact but fragmented and polarized, children and youths may not have any type of bond with any other member of the family. Some of the loneliest children are in families with two parents. The quality of the relationship is the key to the child feeling comfortable in asking for help. If the child is unable to voice the issues or thoughts with which he or she is struggling, depressive thoughts begin to fester.

Blended families present challenges of their own. For some children, the loss of one parent and the introduction of a new one (and possibly new step-siblings) are overwhelming and may trigger a depression. The key to successful blending of families is the amount of openness and communication given during the transition. Transitions must be well planned and sequential in delivery. Moving children into a foreign environment may only accentuate the onset of depression. However, well-planned change, with ongoing discussion about feelings and fears, leads to the possibility of a more successful adaptation. Communication and recognition of fears, and how the fear will be addressed, are important for the child. Telling a child that he or she must accept the new family unit is a tangible formula for depression. Books have been written about the difficulties of step families. The key for the adults is in how they foster the transitions and how they empower their children and youth to accept the change as something that will lead to a good quality of life.

Single-parent households face many challenges. The issues of parental supervision, and quality time, finances, housing, basic needs, and balance of work and family are all sources from which a child can create thoughts and feelings of inadequacy, insecurity, and helplessness. For some single-parent units, the separation from an unstable or unsuitable parent is a blessing, as now there can be a quality of life and safety that did not exist in the intact family unit. Many single parents are overwhelmed with providing the basic necessities of life and often are not aware of the emotional decline of their children. Lack of supervision has been linked as a direct cause of children acting out or seeking comfort in alcohol, drugs, and, in some cases, as runaways. They are unable to live within the present stressful environment and go looking elsewhere for something or someone that may help them feel better. They begin to seek out ways of numbing themselves so that they do not have to accept how poor their quality of life really is. Many, but not all, runaways are byproducts of single-parent households. There are also many single-parent households that are functional. When children of those homes become depressed, parents are mobilized into action and attempt to obtain the best possible service and treatment, no matter what kind of sacrifice needs to be made.

Families with adopted children face myriad issues that may trigger depression. The list may include abandonment and attachment disorders, self-esteem, trust, communication, grief, and adjustment factors. Some adopted children blend well and are an integral part of the adopted family. Others have a sense of searching and longing to know their parental roots and the circumstances of their adoption. The level of communication and honesty on the part of the parents will be paramount in whether the child asks questions and receives satisfactory answers. Some adoptive families have tried to prevent the child from seeking their birth parents. Often this results in enormous personal and family conflict. The prevention of this search will result in depression for many children. The timing of when to begin giving answers or allowing the search for answers is a personal one, and unique to each family.

Experience has taught that trying to bury a child's heritage will only lead to feelings of helplessness and hopelessness, which in turn fosters and fuels depression. Seeking biological parents is as unique as the adopted individual. Some have no interest and never need to know, while others have a sense of longing for information. On many occasions, adopted children are disappointed by what they find in their biological parents. This may also germinate the depression. Some children create a whole fantasy world around the birth parent and are sorely disappointed when the individual has no interest in knowing them. This rejection leads to feelings of abandonment that may have been buried since learning of their adoption.

If children wish to seek birth parents, it is the responsibility of the adoptive parents to facilitate the complex interactions that will make that happen. It must be handled appropriately and gently to assure that the child is able to understand the avalanche of feelings and thoughts that may suddenly come to the forefront in their life. Proper guidance and support is needed to make this process happen so as to avoid a subsequent depression.

There is an increased concern about children not receiving the proper nurturing and, therefore, developing reactive attachment disorders. A lack of bonding may lead to an increased risk of depression. It is key that in the early years a support system is built around nurturance so the child is supported through the several stages of personality development. Failure to do so predisposes the child to depression and other psychopathology such as anxiety, conduct, antisocial, and defiance disorders.

This chapter has discussed the many factors that play prominent roles in the development and treatment of depression or depressive symptoms. The adults in a child's life are paramount to psychological and emotional well-being and development.

Chapter Eight

Sexual Orientation and Depression

Gay youths face the issue of surviving adolescence and developing a positive identity as a lesbian, gay, bisexual, or transgendered person in what is an often hostile and judgmental environment. Contrary to popular belief, adolescence is not always the best time of one's life for many. It is a complex period of development filled with anxiety and only a few clear guidelines for helping adolescents resolve problems. They experience changes in physical, emotional, intellectual, and sexual development. There is no common experience. The experience a child will have with adolescence is as unique as the context of their particular culture, family, peer group, and capacity as individuals.

During troubled times, they must learn who they are, how they fit in, and what their futures may hold for them. Problems in accomplishing these tasks play a critical role in the depressive feelings of any youth, but they present even more hardship for those who are gay or lesbian. Firstly, they must come to understand and accept themselves in a society that provides little positive information about who they are and has negative reactions to their enquiries. Secondly, they must find support among significant others who frequently reject them. Lastly, they must come to terms with their gay identity.

Gay and lesbian adolescents have come to terms with their orientation at an earlier age than ever before. This has placed them in very awkward situations of still living at home, attending schools, and being caught up in a society still grappling with the issues of orientation. Lesbian and gay youths are the most invisible and outcast group of young people in our schools and communities. Many of them attempt to pass as heterosexual in their communities while facing tremendous internal struggles to understand and accept themselves. Many choose to wear a mask and hide their true identities and feelings. They lead a double life rather than confront situations or people that may result in emotional or physical pain. They live in constant fear of being unmasked and recognized as gay or lesbian. The inner battle is one of chaos, fear, and self-loathing.

Gay and lesbian youths are the only groups of adolescents who may face total rejection from their family unit. Many parents are unable to reconcile their child's sexual orientation with their own moral and/or religious values. Several research studies have reported that there was higher incidence of verbal and physical abuse of gay and lesbian youths from parents and siblings than any other youth group. These adolescents were more often forced to leave their homes than others who run away for other reasons.

Openly gay and lesbian youths, or those suspected of being so, may expect harassment and abuse in middle and high school. There is a high rate of suicide among gay and lesbian youths. The shame of ridicule and fear of attack makes school a fearful place, and this results in frequent absences and sometimes, academic failure. Many of these students end up dropping out not because of academic difficulties, but because of the constant threats to their personal safety. Gay and lesbian youths are the only groups of adolescents with no peer group from which to receive support. This lack of support leads to extreme isolation and the loss of close friends. Many schools in North America are unable to address the concerns or affirm the identity of a gay or lesbian adolescent. Students may be subjected to verbal, physical, and even sexual abuse with little recourse. High schools today are attempting to change this by forming gay-straight alliances as a way of trying to support and protect gay and lesbian youths. Even sympathetic teachers and staff often do not know how to relate to gay or lesbian youths or support them in conflicts with other students. Gay and lesbian students often become isolated from, or ignored by, other adolescents and staff who feel uncomfortable with them. The students are easy targets to be turned into scapegoats in efforts to force them to leave school.

The result of this rejection and abuse in all areas of their lives is devastating for gay and lesbian youths. Perhaps the most serious problems they face are emotional ones. When gay and lesbian students are told repeatedly that they are sick, bad, or wrong for being who they are, they eventually begin to believe it. With this constant verbal assault, they frequently internalize a negative image of themselves, and become fearful and withdrawn. More so than other adolescents, they feel utterly alone and often suffer from chronic depression.

In depression, many gay and lesbian youths turn to substance use. Alcohol or drugs serve the functional purposes of reducing the pain and anxiety of external conflicts and reducing the internal inhibitions of homosexual feelings and behavior. Prolonged substance abuse only contributes to the youths' problems and may magnify suicidal feelings.

Substance abuse may, at times, lead to running away, and the resultant homelessness. Gay and lesbian youths enter a further outcast status that presents serious dangers, and an even greater risk of suicide. Without proper educational training, many become involved in prostitution as a means of survival. They face physical and sexual assaults on a daily basis and constant exposure to sexually transmitted diseases, including AIDS. Although it has become easier in recent years to be a gay or lesbian adult, it may be more difficult than ever to be a gay or lesbian youth. With all of the conflicts they face in accepting themselves, such as coming out to families and peers, establishing themselves prematurely in independent living, facing the specter of AIDS, there is a growing danger that their lives are becoming a nightmare.

Many young people face tremendous pressure to desist from any homosexual behavior and develop a heterosexual orientation. It is easy to see why youths with predominately homosexual feelings and experiences try to deny a lesbian or gay identity. They have internalized the image of being homosexual as wrong and dangerous to their physical and mental health. They have seen the stereotypes and do not like them, thus beginning the internal conflict of identification and identity. This chaos can lead to many confusing feelings and emotions, and result in situational depression. The feelings of being all alone and different fuel irrational beliefs about self and forces many gay and lesbian youths to experiment with heterosexual sexual activity. They are pressured to engage in activities that may confuse them even more. Eventually, the adolescent becomes disheartened and manifests depressive and, at times, destructive behaviors, in extreme cases, suicide.

Youths who try to change their homosexual orientation and are unable to do so are at high risk for emotional and behavioral problems. They often develop feelings of hatred and rage that may be turned against themselves or others. They may engage in self-destructive behaviors such as substance abuse as an unconscious expression of feelings too painful to face. Others become involved in verbal and physical attacks against other homosexuals as a way of fighting their own fears. Finally, when the youth comes to recognize for the first time that he or she has a genuinely homosexual orientation, overtly suicidal behavior may result.

Many youths are aware of their gay and lesbian identities but decide not to be open about it to their families and peers and try to pass as heterosexual. They live a lie, and realize that all aspects of their lives are about playing games, and of deception at all levels. They play a role while remaining seemingly invisible. The pain and loneliness of hiding often causes serious harm to their mental health and social development. A serious consequence of this adaptation is that these youth suffer their fears and low-self esteem in silence. Gay and lesbian youths live in perpetual fear that their secret will be discovered. They become increasingly afraid to associate with others and withdraw socially in an effort to avoid what they perceive as a growing number of dangerous situations. They spend more and more time alone, which predisposes them to depression.

A suicidal crisis may be precipitated by a minor event that serves as a last straw to the youth. A low grade may confirm for the youth that life is a failure. An unwitting homophobic remark by parents may be taken to mean that the youth is no longer loved. Perceived rejection is very real for gay and lesbian youths. They expect it and, therefore, are not surprised when it does occur.

Young people who accept their orientation and are open with others form a smaller but visible segment of the gay and lesbian youth population. Once they have accepted their sexual orientation, gay and lesbian youths begin to find where they fit within or outside of the confines of traditional social structures. Gay and lesbian youths usually do not begin to be open about their orientation until middle to late adolescence. They take tremendous risks by being open about who they are. They may experience suicidal feelings because of the pressures they face in conflicts with others about their homosexual orientation and the disappointments they experience at the initial hardships of an openly gay and lesbian orientation.

Gay and lesbian youths of ethnic minorities have all of the problems that other gay and lesbian youths face while growing up in a judgmental society. They also suffer the same economic discrimination and prejudice confronted by other ethnic-minority youths because of racism. The incidence of racism seems to lead to a sense of hopelessness and helplessness that, in turn, leads to increase risk for depression and suicide. They must contend with discrimination and special problems from their own ethnic groups because of sexual orientation. Ostracism and separation from their families and peers is particularly painful and difficult for these youths to cope with.

Two issues that strongly affect gay and lesbian youths of ethnic minorities are religion and family. Ethnic cultures have historically believed that homosexuality is a sin. Parents frequently use religion as the standard by which to evaluate homosexuality. Their gay and lesbian children internalize these religious values, feel guilty for having homosexual feelings and experiences, and fear that they are condemned to hell. The family also plays a central role in the lives of these youths with strong expectations that they will fulfill social roles and perpetuate the family. A homosexual orientation is sometimes seen by the youths as a sign of disrespect to the family and a threat to a family's lineage.

Ethnic minority youths have tremendous fears of losing their extended family and being alone in the world. This fear is exacerbated by the isolation they already face in our society as people of color. Youth of ethnic minorities who are rejected by families are at a risk of depression and suicide because of the tremendous pressures they face in being gay or lesbian, as well as a person of color in a white, homophobic society.

Transsexual youth are, perhaps, the most outcast of all young people and face a grave risk of depressive and suicidal feelings and behavior. These youth believe they have a gender identity different from the sex with which they were born. They often manifest this belief in childhood through an expressed desire to be a person of the opposite gender, rejection of their genitalia, and nonconformity regarding specific gender activities or behaviors. All transsexuals are vulnerable to internalizing an extremely negative image of themselves. They experience tremendous internal conflict between this image and their persistent desire to become the person they believe they are. Transsexuals tend to feel hopelessly trapped. These feelings may be particularly pronounced in young transsexuals who are forced to hide their identity. While wanting to change their sex, they are seldom able to do so and feel condemned to a life they are convinced is a mistake. Transsexuals frequently experience considerable anxiety and depression that the individual may attribute to inability to live in the role of the desired sex. This depression, combined with poor self-esteem, can easily result in suicidal feelings and behaviors in transsexual youth.

Transsexual youth who are open about their identity face extreme abuse and rejection from families and peers. Many are forced to leave their home communities and survive on the streets. Their future in our society is poor, and they are at high risk of suicide. Gender dysphoria is a disorder of which we have little understanding. The only known course of treatment is to help transsexuals adjust to their believed gender identity and undergo gender-reassignment surgery. Most transsexual youths, however, are unable to obtain or afford the help they need in resolving their identity conflicts.

A predisposing factor in depression and suicidal feelings among many adolescents is poor self-esteem. This is especially true for gay and lesbian adolescents who have internalized a harshly negative image of themselves from society, religion, family, and peers. For youths, a poor self-image contributes substantially to a lack of confidence in being able to cope with problems. The images of homosexuals as sick and self-destructive have a huge impact on the coping skills of gay and lesbian youths. Those who have internalized a message throughout their lives of being worthless, and are unable to cope with or escape abusive and chaotic families are also at great risk of depression and suicide.

Youths with poor self-esteem and poor coping skills are particularly vulnerable to depression and suicidal feelings when confronting a problem for the first time. They do not know how to resolve it, or even if they can. Gay youths are highly susceptible to suicidal feelings during the coming-out process.

Many gay and lesbian youths feel trapped in school settings because of a compulsory obligation to attend and the inability to defend themselves against verbal and physical assaults. Schools do not adequately protect gay youths, with teachers often reluctant to stop harassment or rebut homophobic remarks for fear of being seen as undesirable role models. Verbal and physical attacks against gay youths have increased in recent years as students become increasingly threatened by the presence and openness of peers with a lesbian or gay orientation. This abuse begins as early as late elementary school, becomes pronounced in middle school when youths are still markedly immature, and continues into high school. The failure of schools to address this concern can be tragic.

By ignoring the subject in all curricula, including family life classes, schools deny access to positive information about homosexuality that could improve the self-esteem of gay youths. They may also perpetuate myths and stereotypes that condemn homosexuality and deny youths access to positive adult and gay role models. This silence equals tacit support for homophobic attitudes and conduct by some students.

Public and private schools must take responsibility for providing all students at the middle- and high-school level with positive information about homosexuality. Curriculum materials should include information relevant to gays and lesbians as it pertains to human sexuality, health, literature, and social studies. Family life classes should present homosexuality as a natural and healthy form of sexual expression. Information on critical health issues such as AIDS should be presented to all students. Curricula should also include values clarification around social roles to increase the respect for individual differences and reduce the stigma attached to gender nonconformity. A variety of gay and lesbian adult orientation should be presented as positive and viable for youths. All youths should learn about prominent lesbians and gays throughout history. Social-studies courses should include issues relevant to gay and lesbian concerns, and provide youths with positive gay and lesbian adult role models in our society.

Schools need to take responsibility for protecting gay and lesbian youths from abuse from their peers and providing them with a safe environment to receive an education. School staff needs to receive training on how to work and handle conflicts involving gay and lesbian youths.

Teachers should feel secure in being able to rebut homophobic remarks and defend gays youth against harassment. Strong disciplinary actions should be imposed on those who victimize gay and lesbian youths. It is important for schools to hire openly gay and lesbian teachers to serve as role models and resource support for gay and lesbian youth. Counseling services sensitive to the needs and concerns of gay and lesbian youths should be available. Special educational programs may need to be developed for those youths who cannot be incorporated into existing school settings.

The following list is used to measure the risk factors that a gay or lesbian student may encounter that would lead to a likelihood of depression and/or suicidal behavior. Each category lists a variety of conditions or situations or factors that will predispose the onset of a problem for the gay or lesbian child or youth. This list is not exhaustive, as many other factors are not mentioned. This table and list is intended as a guide to build awareness and possible warning signs for the adults in the lives of gay and lesbian youth.

General Risk Factors

1. Awareness and identification of homosexual orientation at an early age.
2. Self-acceptance of homosexual orientation.
3. Conflicts with others related to homosexual orientation.
4. Problems in homosexual relationships.

Societal Risk Factors

1. Discrimination and oppression of homosexuals by the child's society.
2. Portrayal of homosexuals as self-destructive by the individual's society.

Self-Esteem Risk Factors

1. Internalization of image of homosexuals as sick or bad.
2. Internalization of image of homosexuals as helpless and self-destructive.

Identity Conflicts Risk Factors

1. Denial of homosexual orientation.
2. Despair in recognition of homosexual orientation.

Family Risk Factors

1. Rejection of child because of homosexual orientation.
2. Abuse/harassment of child because of homosexual orientation.
3. Failure of child to meet parental/social expectation.
4. Perceived rejection of child because of homosexual orientation.

Religion Risk Factors

1. Child's homosexual orientation seen as incompatible with family's religious beliefs.
2. Youth feels sinful and condemned to hell because of homosexual orientation.

School Risk Factors

1. Abuse/harassment of homosexual youth by peers.
2. Lack of accurate information about homosexuality.

Social Isolation Risk Factors

1. Rejection of homosexual youth by friends and peers.
2. Social withdrawal of homosexual youth.
3. Loneliness and inability to meet others like the youth.

Substance Abuse Risk Factors

1. Substance use to relieve pain of oppression.
2. Substance use to reduce inhibitions of homosexual feelings.

Professional Help Risk Factors

1. Refusal of the helping professional to accept homosexual orientation of youth.
2. Involuntary treatment to change homosexual orientation of youth.
3. Inability to discuss issues related to homosexuality.

Residential Program Risk Factors

1. Refusal to accept and support homosexual orientation of youth.
2. Isolation of homosexual youth by staff and residents.
3. Inability to support homosexual youth in conflicts with residents.

Relationship Problems Risk Factors

1. Inability to develop relationship skills like heterosexual youth.
2. Extreme dependency needs because of prior emotional deprivation.
3. Absence of social supports in resolving relationship conflicts.

Independent Living Risk Factors

1. Lack of support from family.
2. Lack of support from adult gay and lesbian community.
3. Involvement with street life (prostitution, homelessness).

AIDS Risk Factors

1. Unsafe sexual practices.
2. Secrecy and unplanned nature of early sexual experiences.

Future Outlook Risk Factors

1. Despair of future life, belief life will be as hard as the present.
2. Absence of positive adult gay or lesbian role models.

Source: Adapted from Lambda.org.

It is crucial to understand that these risk factors may be manifested in many different ways and are unique to the individual. It is a guide to build more sensitivity and awareness on the part of the adults in a child's life. Many of these risk factors may manifest themselves as depressive symptoms, and the warnings need to be addressed as soon as possible.

Young people have difficulty seeing a future that is different from the present. Gay and lesbian youths fear their lives will always be as unhappy and as difficult as they presently are. They do not know if they will receive any more caring, acceptance, and support than they are getting now. The little information that they have about homosexuality usually reinforces these mistaken beliefs. Gay and lesbian youths do not understand what life could be like as a gay or lesbian adult. They do not have accurate information about homosexuality, positive role models after which to model themselves, or knowledge of adult gay and lesbian communities. They frequently do not know that many gay and lesbian adults lead stable, happy, prosperous, and productive lives. They go through adolescence feeling lonely, afraid, and hopeless. Sometimes they take their own lives.

The lack of information about youth gay and lesbian depression and suicide is a reflection of the oppression of homosexuals by our society and the invisibility of large numbers of gay and lesbian adults as perceived by the youth population. There is growing awareness that a serious problem exists, but we have only started to break down the silence surrounding the issue.

Comprehensive research is needed to determine the extent and nature of depression and suicide among gay and lesbian youths. These studies must ensure that the entire spectrum of gay and lesbian youth is adequately represented, including gays, lesbians, homeless youths, and ethnic minorities. This research can be the foundation for greater recognition of the problem and the allocation of resources designed to address it. Hopefully, the work done in recent years will serve as a helpful beginning toward ending depression and suicide among gay and lesbian youths.

Chapter Nine

Personnel Needed for Support

The personnel needed in working with depressed students can be as simple as a caring parent or as extensive as a team of mental-health professionals. The level of dysfunction of the child determines the level of involvement in the treatment process.

If unsure where to go for help, check the yellow pages of the telephone directory under mental health, health, social services, suicide prevention, crisis-intervention services, hotlines, hospitals, or physicians for phone numbers and addresses. In times of crisis, the emergency-room physician at a hospital may be able to provide temporary help for an emotional problem and give advice on professional follow-up. Many professionals can provide assistance. Some of the people listed will be able to provide or make a referral, diagnosis, and/or possibly offer treatment services.

The first line of defense is your family physician. She or he has a family history and has probably seen the child since birth and has knowledge of the physical health of the child. Be careful not to assume that your general practitioner can diagnose depression. He or she is more likely to recognize the physical aspects of the depression. The physician may prescribe medication, which may alter or only mask the symptoms. However, it is necessary to obtain a referral to a mental-health practitioner trained to work with a child or adolescent who is manifesting depression.

The school guidance counselor is another good resource if the depression is reactional or situational. School can be a wonderful place for children, but it can also be a source of great stress and anxiety. The fear of failure and being socially rejected or isolated may lead to depression manifesting itself within the classroom. This professional can provide coping skills, management skills, and problem-solving skills that can empower the child or adolescent to be less reactive in the school setting. The child can learn new ways of being included, communicating, and voicing his or her concerns in a way that will lead to proactive change. Contact with a school counselor may prevent academic failure. He or she can also be a liaison to the rest of the school faculty and communicate your concerns so as not to aggravate the situation for the child. The school nurse is another daily resource for the child. The nurse will dispense medications if necessary, but may also provide some well-needed care, nurturing, and/or daily advice and attention.

A paraprofessional or para-educator is often found in the classroom and works primarily with children with special needs. That person may also form a close emotional bond with the child and be a support within the classroom by facilitating and managing the daily workload and helping the child maneuver academics and homework.

Psychiatrists are also key in the treatment of depression. They are medical doctors who provide both physical and mental evaluations. Many psychiatrists follow a specific treatment modality, so it is important to ask specific questions about what modality they employ. Psychiatrists believe that depression is chemically based and is treated by medication alone. The best treatments are those that combine both medication and talk therapy (cognitive behavioral therapy). Be wary of those who only refill prescriptions, as is sometimes the case for adults.

Psychologists serve as very useful resources for treating depression. They are generally based more in therapy than in medication. There a few states that allow psychologists to prescribe antidepressants. Generally speaking, the majority of these professionals follow a therapeutic model as well. Many psychologists will follow one or a combination of the following approaches. The four main approaches are: social skills, self-control, helplessness, and cognitive strategies. These approaches will be discussed later in the treatment section.

Social workers are often included in the treatment of depressed children because of the effects that depressed children may have on the dynamics of families. They provide some community services for both parent and child. They access services that may provide financial, emotional, medical, and other basic needs for the family that is distraught by the fact that their depressed child is creating enormous chaos.

Mental-health counselors can also provide support and therapy for the child as well as for the family. Many counselors are licensed and regulated. They cannot prescribe medications but may make referrals to physicians. Health-maintenance organizations often pay for services of one of these professionals. It is important to check whether one's health policy will pay for the counseling visits and/or cover some of the prescriptions. At times the bureaucracy may be daunting; however, with determination, one can ensure that the depression of the child and the accompanying costs do not overwhelm the family and create more stress or worry.

Community mental-health centers also offer services for individuals and families. Centers offer specialized programs that deal with grief, depression, addictions, etc. It is vital to find a center that will provide services that recognize the specific needs of a depressed child. Many centers do very well with adults, however, they are less efficient in dealing with children. Find a center that specializes in children and is better able to deliver quality programming meant for that specific audience.

Hospital psychiatry departments and outpatient clinics are another source of support if the child or adolescent may need to be admitted to the hospital because of a risk of committing suicide. They provide 24-hour supervision and health care. They are often a lock-up facility, and provide short-term solutions for a child in crisis. University or medical-school-affiliated programs include the client as training for their medical students. A depressed child can receive treatment free of charge, but he or she would be required to agree to be a teaching model for student medical practitioners. These practitioners are supervised and often can deliver quality programming. This is a viable option to lower-income families, provided there is one nearby.

Private clinics and facilities provide services for depressed individuals; however, they tend to be expensive. Many of these institutions run quality programs that may cost thousands of dollars. Very few offer short-term treatment plans and usually cater to the population that can afford them. They follow a variety of treatment modalities and are located throughout the United States. Many offer residential facilities.

Employee assistance programs are another source of help. Many individuals have these programs at work. These plans offer short-term help (usually to a maximum of six visits) with a professional within their network of service providers. This is often a great beginning to discussion of the possibility that depression may be affecting the whole family. Usually, once the allotted visits have been used, a referral is made to a local provider, and the family or individual decides whether to continue with the treatment or to explore other options.

Clergy have also been trained in mental-health counseling and can offer support for the individual and/or family, depending on the family's spiritual beliefs. Clergy cannot prescribe medication, but can offer spiritual guidance and possibly different perspectives on the life events occurring at that moment. This type of help would be excellent for situational depressions but ineffective for biochemical depressions that require medications to alter the functioning in the brain.

The appendix contains a list of many organizations and service providers in all American states. If one is seeking help, begin the investigation with the list. Individuals and organizations are able to provide help and services. There is no reason to deal with depression in secret. There are solutions.

Chapter Ten

What Teachers Can Do

A child's functioning can vary greatly at different times of the day, season, and school year. Flexibility on the part of the teacher is crucial. Teachers may see aspects of a child's behavior, aspects a parent does not have the opportunity to observe. Teachers notice how children interact with other children and how they act when alone.

Teachers need to learn about mood disorders and the side effects of treatments prescribed for the student. At times, well-meaning teachers have aggravated the situation because they were unaware that a child was suffering from a major depression.

Identification and reducing stressors within a classroom makes the atmosphere safer and more palatable. Teachers set the pace and climate, and knowing what triggers the child may reduce the amount of depressive behavior on the part of the child. The teacher must be aware of sensory overload and help manage it in a way that does not overwhelm the child. In turn, the child is more likely to remain productive and involved in the daily routine of the classroom.

Teacher awareness around the issues of boredom, bullying, homework, and competition will provide succor for the depressed child. The child is already depressed, and increased stressors of bullying may push the child into depression. Schools and teachers need to have zero tolerance for this type of behavior. Teasing, taunting, and/or name calling may also be symptomatic of a child who feels depressed and thus takes out his or her frustration on others in the hope that they will be as miserable as he or she is.

Teachers also need to be aware that homework may not be done because the child is unable to motivate himself or herself to do it or just cannot summon any energy to do anything beyond attending school. Punishing a depressed student for unfinished homework just makes the child feel more of a failure. Depressed children do not compete well. Since they already feel poorly about themselves, losing at games and contests only reinforces the fact that they cannot cope. This type of activity needs to be used with caution by giving the depressed child the choice of not being involved. Many teachers see the refusal to participate as defiance, when it is actually a coping strategy for survival.

Teachers are encouraged to do referrals for psycho-educational testing, while the school system must take the referral seriously and have a team of professionals investigate the situation. It is suggested that teachers record observations and collect data on a daily basis so as to pass on this information to the referral team and/or the school psychologist. The following is a list of criteria that a teacher can use to collect data and evidence:

- depressed and/or irritable mood lasting more than two weeks
- change in appetite or weight, in small children failure to make appropriate weight gain
- too active or not active enough
- deliberately misbehaves in school
- loss of interest in school and school activities
- social withdrawal, feels left out, openly reject friends
- drop in grades
- loss of energy or chronic fatigue and/or sleeping in class
- anxiety ranging from assorted vague worries about the future to paralyzing delusional fears
- difficulty concentrating on assignments or indecision
- unable to store new information
- unable to retrieve what she or he already knows
- forgotten materials and assignments
- inappropriate guilt
- low self-esteem, says feel dumb, can't do anything right, disappoint others
- frequent absences, trips to clinics, comments on not feeling well
- hearing voices inside their head or out, when no one else is around
- crying in class

- writes about hopelessness, death, and suicide themes in assignments and/or notes, and/or talks about suicide in class.

Once this checklist has been completed, share the results with the guidance counselor and parents so that a team approach between teachers, counselor, and parents may be planned to help the child.

After completing the checklist, talk to parents to let them know what has been observed. Talk in specifics. By so doing, the teacher is talking about the content, not the child. Establish a baseline of communication by asking the parents if there is anything they can share on how to help their child's situation. Stress that teachers do not feel the child's depression reflects upon the parents. Sometimes, the student can be helped just by the parent conferences and, other times, by taking a step beyond. The steps include utilizing and talking with other school staff (such as a psychologist, a guidance counselor, other teachers, and/or a principal).

In the classroom, the teacher can work out a signal that the student can use, meaning it is not a good day, the student is not feeling well, or the student is starting to cry. A teacher may notice students do not appear to be taking their medicine and ask, "Did you take your medication today?" Students can be encouraged to accept all kinds of differences in people, and not only medical differences. When a friend talks about committing suicide, tell students to inform a trusted adult who can help avert a tragedy.

Teachers can also help identify a person and place at school to which the child can go if symptoms become overwhelming. Having this predetermined safe zone for students helps them save face if they are experiencing a serious episode or a breakdown. This zone can be the nurse's or counselor's office, places where the child can feel totally safe physically and emotionally.

Children with depression are often tardy and absent because of fatigue, anxiety, depression, and other symptoms. They must not be punished for being late. Loss of recess or detentions will not cure the tardiness. It is important for the teacher to use good judgment and common sense when deciding what work the child will make up. Doing every single piece of work will only discourage the child more and may lead to more absences. The child will see the mountain of work and will believe that there is no way he or she can catch up, and absences may become more frequent.

Once teachers are trained, they soon realize that there are many different options to working with depressed children. A low speaking voice and a calm demeanor are more effective than confrontation. Children with depression are more likely to regress and/or become withdrawn if yelled at or confronted. They are already unable to cope with their daily stress. The additional stress of an angry adult will only force them to pull away.

Communication between home and school, as previously noted, is imperative in helping the child in both settings. This can be achieved in many different ways, such as back-and-forth notebooks that document the day's challenges, victories, successes, incidents, and generally encouraging comments. Telephone calls (such as sunshine calls) can really be inspiring for a depressed child, and for an overwhelmed parent. Technology can also be used, e-mails that give positive and encouraging feedback. Negative e-mails only add to the complexity of the already difficult situation. Teachers can provide feedback for change and improvement; however, it is recommended that the e-mail begin positively, offer constructive feedback, and end positively.

Something as simple as unlimited access to drinking water and bathroom breaks can have a major impact. Water is a calming agent to combat some of the internal dialogue and stress. Being hydrated helps the individual focus and concentrate at the task at hand. Being able to go to the bathroom is not dramatic in itself, but withdrawing from a stressful environment for a short period of time may be enough to help the child work through whatever is causing chaos. Allowing depressed students this leeway will give them the chance to sift away some of the difficulties that they may be trying to work through on their own.

School can be a wonderful place for children to express ideas, concerns, and fears in a variety of ways. Teachers should encourage expression and learning in these areas through art, music, and creative writing. Art is an excellent way for children to express some of their deepest fears and concerns. The art and the interpretation of the drawings can lead to insights about the child's pain and inner turmoil. If a piece of art is of concern, the educator should share it with parents, a counselor, or a psychologist. Music has a soothing effect on depressed children. Thus, allowing a child access to music may be the calming agent required to prevent a child from falling apart. Small headsets allow the individual to escape and work at becoming centered again so as to be able to return to the normal functioning of the daily classroom routine.

Creative writing can be a vehicle for expression of intense feelings either through poetry, journal writing, or short stories. Students will often allow the words to flow as a way of channeling the emotions onto paper. Giving the emotions voice seems to release many bottled-up emotions. Analysis of the writing and the style used can lead to insights about what the author is feeling or experiencing. Writing can also be used to springboard discussions in a therapeutic relationship, or with teacher and parent.

Teachers need to understand that a depressed child will often experience lower grades because of the inability to complete assignments. There must be a level of flexibility with assignments, homework, and testing techniques. Homework may not be completed regularly because of the cycle of moods. Being aware of the episodes and employing some level of modification of expectations will lead to a better chance that the homework will be completed. Testing is another area of great concern for depressed students, especially if they have missed many parts of the material and feel unprepared to take the test. Instead of setting up the child for failure, provide the necessary supports and direct instruction before giving the test. The results are much more likely to be truly indicative of the child's ability.

Children with depression do not transition well because of the fear of change and of the unknown. For smoother transitions, allow extra time and give advance notice before each change in staffing or routine. They need predictability and structure. They function on the known. The routine must remain the same because it signals a level of safety and routine. Changing the routine accelerates stress and anxiety. If an unforeseen change will occur, there must be advance notice to the child.

Teachers can be great observers in a classroom. It is fundamentally important that educators be aware of changes that signal relapse. Ongoing communication with parents and medical professionals is necessary so that the educator can signal any type of change to the necessary support systems. Guidance counselors and teachers can form a wonderful alliance in informing all the students in their classes about what depression is and how it can affect learning and life. Morning meetings are helpful in discussing what sadness is and how one sometimes feels blue or always tired. Depending on the age of the child, the proper vocabulary needs to be used to describe the difficult components of depression. Talking about depression at school creates an open environment. It no longer has to be a secret pain that a child or adolescent must endure in silence.

Chapter Eleven

What Parents Can Do

Parenting a child with a depressive disorder is not an easy burden to bear. Often, depression may be a lifelong struggle for both child and parent. It is imperative that parents learn about mood disorders, treatments and services available, and any combination of illnesses the child may have in conjunction with the depression.

Coping with depression at home will be a challenge. It is crucial for parents to remember that their parenting did not cause the child's depression. If the depression is situational, a series of events may have triggered depressive episodes. If the depression is chemical, it is a problem with the functioning of the brain and not the fault of either parent. It is fundamental in the management of the depression that the parent(s) continue to use hugs and soothing words to calm a child. They may be very insecure or unsure of what is happening, so it is important that physical touch be part of the relationship. Encourage exercise as a means of improving depressive symptoms. Being outside or doing physical activity may stimulate the brain to release more endorphins and, thus, improve mood. Do not force a child to partake in an activity if he or she finds it extremely difficult or unappealing.

When speaking with the child, use positive feedback to point out the times he or she has done something that made him or her feel better. The purposes of this strategy are to help the child begin to generalize the good feelings and experiences, and diminish the focus on the negative events or situations.

Sleeping is another area about which a parent needs to be concerned. Supervise the child's sleep habits to ensure adequate sleep, or to notice oversleeping in adolescents. Excessive sleep often manifests itself as one of the symptoms. There are a variety of calming aids (such as herbal tea, massages, and reading stories) that help a child who has difficulty in falling and staying asleep.

Ongoing, open communication is very important in encouraging the child to talk to friends and family about thoughts and feelings. The more the child does this, the more he or she can unload and process some of the negative thoughts that could be pulling her or him into deeper depressive symptoms. The ability to verbalize one's fears and feel heard are paramount in any recovery program or, at the very least, a management plan for depression. Medication is often used for children with depression. It is important to supervise that any medication is taken regularly and properly. Many children stop taking their medication once they begin to feel better and, thus, the effect of the medication is not used to its fullest potential.

Children who write in a diary about their good and bad days seem to cope better overall. When they are feeling down and overwhelmed they can go back and read about their good days. Parents also should keep a daily diary of the child's mood, energy, behaviors, statements of concern, treatment responses, and sleep. These observations can be key when speaking with a physician, counselor, teacher, or mental-health professional. Do not rely on your memory. Use specific documentation as a way to monitor progress or regression. The diary can serve as an accurate reminder of the wins and losses. This diary can also be used to chart responses to specific interventions.

Communication with the school is paramount in helping teachers understand the level at which the child is functioning. It is helpful to write a letter to teachers and counselors explaining the child's illness, how it affects the child, and if medication needs to be dispensed by them. Explain the medicine's side effects and what symptoms they should report to the parent. If the child has a problem with sleeplessness, arrange that the child's most difficult classes be in the afternoon so the student can sleep in. This is much easier to accommodate at the middle and high school levels. The understanding will be that the child would be responsible for any missed work, and a formula or plan would be devised to ensure that this would occur without overwhelming the child/adolescent.

Have the child evaluated by a child psychiatrist with experience in early-onset mood disorders. An evaluation will either confirm or negate the existence of the depression, and will aid in taking appropriate forms of action. A neuropsychologist or educational psychologist may evaluate the child for hidden learning disabilities that may be or are causing stress at school. Learning disabilities are often found in children with depression. Once the learning disability is discovered, it can be programmed for, and modifications can be made to help ensure the child's success.

Depression is a multilayered disorder that is manifested in many different ways. It can have a continuum of reactions and responses. Parents must prioritize symptoms and address them in order of severity. Do not try to address all of them at the same time. The child or adolescent will become even more withdrawn because of the perception of failure and incompetence. Choose less severe symptoms and help the child master them with appropriate techniques and strategies that will lead to corrective and productive changes. For example, helping the child maintain a routine for sleep, mealtimes, and activities, can give him or her a sense of accomplishment and control over his or her life. Because of the fact that many stressors are not known until the child speaks of them, anticipate or avoid stressful situations. Limit frightening movies and television shows, and be prepared to leave events early as necessary. At times, the feelings of being overwhelmed gradually build up, but, at other times, they will manifest themselves immediately and externally in the form of crying or a demanding to go home. Some triggers may be bright lights, noise, large stores, and groups, which can be over-stimulating and overwhelming.

Once the child is home, use gentle music, relaxation tapes, dim lights, warm baths, and massage to help with the calming, and eventually, sleep. The importance of how the parent responds to the event or situation will lead to a decrease or magnification of the responses. Pets can play an interesting role in the management of depressed children, as they have a therapeutic effect and will often calm the child. The closeness between the animal and the child creates a bond that may resemble a confidant role to the depressed child. Many children talk of their problems to their pet.

There are several protective and preventative strategies available to parents of depressed children and adolescents. The first is effective parental communication. How the adults speak to one another and to their children will either close or open doors. If a child believes that her or his parents can speak about the issues or problems without losing their calm or patience, it will have a direct effect on whether the child reaches out to them in time of need. Many parents want their children to talk to them; however, that is not always possible because of the parent's communication style. If the parent is perceived as judgmental or punishing, the child will avoid communication. Their depressive disorder makes them even more sensitive to tone, voice level, and non-verbal signs of communication.

Second, the strategy of regular meals as a family seems elementary, as a family eating together regularly gives the child a sense of consistency and stability. It is a predictable routine in which family members can share their day's events, challenges, and successes.

Third, when a child acts out, it is important to validate the feelings, but it is not acceptable to express the feelings in an unsafe, aggressive, or violent way that puts other family members in danger. The child is asked to express his or her feelings in clear ways, and hopefully get some resolution or understanding. At no time should it become a war of words, as the child will only act up more or withdraw totally (and become mute about his or her feelings). The combination of expectations and openness needs to be a fine line. It is only by experimenting that a parent can understand the rules for dealing with chaotic situations.

Fourth, the expectations parents have of their children can be a great guiding light, or an extreme source of stress. Expectations need to be appropriate to age and ability. The discussions on expectations should be ongoing and open. Parents must try to understand the level of skill the child may or may not have. For example, expectations of high grades may not be possible during the depressive episodes, but a grade of B or C may be more realistic. Communicating the expectations in a way that makes the latter attainable and realistic is more likely to have positive outcomes. Unrealistic expectations only compound the situation via more complex reactions. Parents who are unable to voice or negotiate realistic expectations close the door to their children. Depressed children do not try to communicate. They just do not bother trying. It is up to the adult to make sure that communication remains open.

Fifth, parental monitoring is crucial in ensuring that the child is where he or she needs or should be. Within this area, there are several questions parents need to ask themselves, or areas that they need to be aware of when dealing with depressed children. This list of questions is not exhaustive, but is meant as a guide to begin the communication.

1. Do you know who your teen's friends are?
2. If your teen is going to be late, does he or she know to call?
3. Do you know what your teen is doing after school?
4. Does your teen tell you whom he or she will be with before going out?
5. Do you know where your teen is when he or she goes out at night?
6. Do you know how your teen spends his or her money?
7. Do you know the parents of your teen's friends?
8. Do you talk with your teen about their plans with friends?

These questions may be self-explanatory, but many parents fail to ask them. They are an excellent way of truly monitoring the activities of adolescents. Checking in with the adolescent frequently may prevent the experimentation of alcohol and drugs, fraternization with undesirable peers, or criminal activity. It also protects adolescents from being taken advantage sexually, emotionally, and, possibly, financially by older adolescents or adults. Many depressed adolescents will seek attention in many different ways, some of those ways being self-destructive.

Sixth, regular communication with school and teachers will prevent problems from accelerating, and many may often be discovered quickly. Failing grades and uncompleted homework and assignments can be addressed before they become a major issue. Ongoing communication can also help in making school officials aware of changes in the depression, or of some of its manifestations. The school can sometimes make adaptations that may alleviate some of the difficulties and stressors for the child. It is only in communicating that problems may be averted. Since children and adolescents go to school as their job, it is important to ensure that they are successful at it.

Seventh, keep the computer in a public space. Depressed adolescents have a habit of isolating themselves in their rooms and of spending many hours on the computer. With the advance in technology and instant messaging, chat rooms, and web cams, students can speak with anyone, anywhere, at anytime. Depressed students who are feeling isolated or who have low self-esteem may be more vulnerable to people who have only prurient intentions and interests. Many pedophiles are seeking just this type of child, one who will offer little to no resistance. Some depressed children will communicate with these individuals because of a false sense of trust and security that they think they have with the predator. There are documented cases of abductions in which children have gone to the mall to meet someone. Parental monitoring of the computer, of those to whom the child communicates, and for how long, may save the child's life.

Eighth, if there are problems in the family around the issue of depression and counseling has been suggested, advise that the parents go first. It is more important that parents have an excellent initial perspective on the issues before addressing them with the child. The parent may be uninformed about the disorder, and a modicum of knowledge becomes an excellent source by which to change dynamics and encounters, and/or stressors for the child and the entire family. Once the parents have received education, counseling, or therapy on the issues, it helps the child to see that treatment is not a process to fear. Parents are coached by the professional to respond with certain words and/or actions. In so doing, the reactions are much more empowering and much less reactive.

Parents want to find joy in their children. Parents need to remind their children of the pleasure and pride that they take in them. Parents must also lavish attention and interest in their children's lives so as to communicate the message that they want to be an integral part of their children's lives. Briefly look in on them while they are doing homework, and show interest and affection. Sometimes, a five-minute conversation as a check-in can lead to great results.

A suggestion that reaps great rewards is one in which parents spend time, not money, on their children. Too often, parents believe they are giving their child everything when, in fact, they are giving what the child does not truly want. All children want is their parents' time and closeness. Parents get too caught up in the busy world to notice that their children need them. The role of the family in the successful treatment of the depressed child or adolescent is crucial. Family counseling has been proven to be a major influence in the recovery and management of some disorders. In many instances, parenting training and education can benefit the family and help prevent depression and other problems. Parents should never underestimate their roles or their power in helping a child recover from depression.

Thus far, the focus has been on what the parent can do for their child or adolescent with depression. The discussion will now focus on what parents will want to do for themselves.

Ignore critical comments by well-meaning friends, relatives, and strangers. These individuals do not know what you are feeling. Their misconceptions about depression and the accompanying statements may, at times, make things worse. Some parents may try to teach and thus inform these individuals, and others may not.

Having a depressed child can sap precious energy. What have you got in place to re-energize? What kinds of self-care strategies do you practice regularly? Exercising, eating right, and getting enough sleep will all boost your energies to keep abreast of the ongoing battles with child or adolescent depression.

If parents are not coping well, they should seek help if they cannot eat or sleep, or they develop anxiety or mood symptoms. It is common for many parents to become ill themselves when dealing with a depressed child. Parents ideally should have access to respite care, or share the responsibility with your partner or other family members.

The medical world is full of varying strategies and treatments for depression. Trust your instincts, and get a second or third opinion if a professional's advice does not make sense to you.

Above all in this journey, maintain a sense of hope. Find some solace, spirituality or creative outlets. Find ways to keep your identity flourishing in this time of extreme chaos. Do activities to enhance your mood, or to help you feel distracted, even for a short while. If parents do not have any of these outlets, they risk inviting mental and physical breakdown. Lastly, find a support group and/or other parents of children who have mood disorders. This can be a source of great support. It will all depend on the type of group you find. Not all groups are healthy, so choose carefully.

Society is often quick to blame parents for how their children turn out, or how they adapt to society's norms and rules. In the case of depression, much of what is happening is beyond the control of most parents. It is only via increased awareness and knowledge that depression will become understood by society. Hopefully, with more awareness, mental-health issues will be received with more of an open mind, and thus, more tolerance.

Chapter Twelve

Strategies to Consider for Depression in the Classroom

Meeting the needs of a student with depression can be a challenge for many educators who may not know exactly what to do. Often, educators are well meaning but misinformed. This chapter will provide strategies and academic instructional modifications and adaptations that with hope will lead to better experiences for these students and teachers within classroom and school settings.

First, teachers can set the pace and climate of their classrooms by establishing reasonable goals. Is the teacher truly aware of what the student can accomplish? Does he or she need to realign the standards or expectations for the student? A good strategy to employ is to provide specific feedback in a non-hostile, non-judgmental, constructive way. If students receive feedback that recognizes their effort as well as their abilities, that student is more likely to continue with a consistent effort to finish the task at hand.

Students with depression are capable of handling responsibility. The adult involved needs to identify what the child's abilities are. The teacher or adult can give responsibility, but knowing the amount and what it constitutes is vital to the success of the child and the situation. All human beings like to be recognized for their efforts. Teaching students to reinforce themselves when they have met their goals, accomplished difficult tasks, or achieved even trivial matters is of great importance. Students live with disappointment and need to have something to look forward to so that motivation can survive.

Students with depression live in a world of darkness and solitude and often do not have a chance to demonstrate their skills or talents in a way that may help them receive accolades for these talents. Educators giving students a chance to show their strengths is a step in the right direction toward building the student's confidence and self-esteem. Helping them recognize and acknowledge these strengths may give them the self-esteem to complete a task or realize a goal.

Time is a gift one can give a depressed child. Removing the pressure of time limit can give the child the time to process the information. The extension of time, however, should be monitored carefully so that the child is productive and not procrastinating. Use word banks or alternative testing methods to accommodate for retrieval problems. On many occasions, children cannot find the proper words to express what they are feeling or wanting to say. Having this word bank nearby will help the child to guide his or her thinking and/or help his or her memory.

Problems of concentration and focus are part of being depressed. Educators can provide refocusing assistance and prompts to keep the child within the classroom context mentally. For some students, seeing the whole assignment may prove to be insurmountable. Break tasks into one- or two-step sequences and confer frequently with the student. If the task is seen as manageable, it is more likely to be completed. If the child feels overwhelmed by the amount of work, dividing it up in smaller pieces makes it more attainable and realistic. Because of the fact that many children with depression miss daily details, it is advised that the educator provide supervision to see that assignments are recorded completely and accurately, and that all materials are packed in the school bag. This extra two minutes of monitoring can prevent a family or student meltdown once the child is at home and is about to do his or her homework. Ensuring that all materials are present also helps the child to stay on par with his or her peers, and not fall far behind in uncompleted work.

Organization is a challenge for depressed students, as often they are in their own world and will forget materials and books at school. If possible, provide a set of books to be left at home during the time the illness is more pronounced. It will alleviate stress for you the educator, the parent, and the child. Homework is a primary component of education, but also a source of extreme stress for many students, regardless if they have depression or not. For some students, homework creates situational depression because of conflict associated with it. Homework may need to be reduced and modified to a more manageable level. Discussion with teacher, student, and parent is paramount in achieving an understanding as to what kinds of modifications will be made, and why. Clear expectations (especially in terms of amount) should be clarified, as should the role each will play in the completion of it.

Placement within the classroom is important. Preferential seating near the teacher and/or positive role model can prevent some acting out. If the teacher or peer is nearby, the student can ask for help without attracting the attention of other students. The teacher may also notice any changes in mood and functioning quickly and address it immediately rather than reacting to the incident, or trying to soothe the child after the fact. The level of connection that a depressed child needs is much higher than that of a non-depressed student. There is need for added support and supervision during transitions and less structured activities. Transitions can become overwhelming when the student does not know where to go, what to do, or what is expected. Therefore, he or she panics, cries or withdraws and becomes totally unresponsive.

In-school counseling and support is one of the fundamental strategies to have in place. The child needs to have a place or person to which or whom he or she is connected, one who really understands what he or she is going through and can guide them through any episodes. This safe zone is a sanctuary that is instrumental in de-escalating the episodes. For some individuals, being in a support group gives their disorder a voice and normalizes them in the face of their peers. It also will confirm that they are not alone. Allowing the student to leave the class as needed, to go to a safe place or safe person in the building may help the child to cope with the depression or the presenting trigger. However, it is important the child not use this strategy as an excuse to avoid work or conflict. It is meant as a support, not an escape mechanism.

Classroom modifications can be done in three areas: environmental, academic, and instructional.

Environmental adaptations are changes that can be done within the physical context of the classroom. A major change is to maintain a brightly lit area and use as much natural light as possible. The more natural light available the less the lethargy and sadness because of the somber feel of the fluorescent lights. Establish a safe place both in the classroom and in an area to retreat when the student becomes overwhelmed. Set up a discrete signal so that the student can leave to a safe place without bringing attention to himself or herself.

As discussed previously, preferred seating near a door away from distractions is a good place. Be flexible about the child's workspace and movement about the classroom. Giving the child permission to move may help him or her to process an emotion as he or she moves, and upon returning to the desk the student can now refocus and get back on task.

Academic modifications are the second area that can lead to proactive changes and help the child feel more successful with the work they need to accomplish and learn. On a daily basis, provide notes to help with attention, or for lateness because of sleep disorder, or frustration with certain tasks; they can help the communication between you the educator and the parent. Miscommunication often leads to conflict, which in turn only enhances the strained relationship between some children and parents.

Workload is another area that needs adjustment. Reduce homework, extend deadlines, adjust assignments, limit stress, and accommodate for alert and non-alert times. Knowing when the child is functioning at a higher level will lead to more productivity.

Evaluation is also another area of concern for depressed students, as the fear of failure is so real and imminent for many. Grade work on the basis of production, not completeness. For example, if he or she completed 10 out of 20 problems, grade the 10 problems and give credit for work done. If the child sees a passing grade instead of a constant failing grade, he or she is more likely to accept future tasks. Giving this child failing grades only confirms to the student that he or she will never be able to be successful.

Testing in this age is everywhere. Students are tested by state and federal agencies in the educational world. Many of these students do not do well in timed, standardized tests. To alleviate some of the stress, give students extended time, word banks, and multiple choices, or oral or alternative assessment. Do the testing in a separate location so that the child can focus. Helping the child tape or dictate their answers may allow them to truly express what they know. Allow the child to leave the testing site for small breaks so that he or she can refocus or go to the bathroom, as some of the medications do have health side effects. Since sleep affects performance, it is necessary to schedule testing at times that the child is most focused and alert.

One way to help in the completion of tasks is to provide a resource room with assignments and materials if the student should need special-education services. Working between the two departments can facilitate learning that would not normally have occurred in the regular general-education classroom. The special-education teacher can break down large projects with frequent check-ins. This can also be used by the general-education teacher.

Instructional modifications in the classroom can drive the success or failure of the depressed child. There are several strategies that can be implemented as part of a teacher's regular functions. Monitor the student for focus and on-task behaviors, as it is very easy for a depressed child to daydream. Monitor the student to confirm assignments are recorded, and all materials are packed and organized. It is important that you take the time to teach organizational skills, as these skills may be crucial for daily functioning.

Maintain open communication with the student so as to be a liaison about the student's changing status, especially around the issue of medications. Medications may affect the level and amount of learning that is realistically achievable. Involve and empower students to show them that they are being heard. This connection is a lifeline to helping the child embrace necessary skills. Providing individual assistance only reinforces the child's belief that you are interested in what he or she is doing. The child sees you as an aide who will guide, but not correct forcefully.

Set up the student for success. Do you as the educator believe that the child can learn and be successful? Having faith and projecting that faith motivates the child to try to succeed. Provide many instances for positive statements and reinforcements. Children need this reinforcement frequently. At the beginning, serve ample praise and then streamline it so as to achieve the necessary outcomes. Peers in the classroom can play an instrumental role in helping in the area of modifications. Assign him or her an empathetic buddy and/or someone who is non-judgmental and caring. This individual can be a peer chosen by the student himself or through the suggestion of the teacher and/or guidance counselor. This individual needs to be strong, understanding, aware, instinctive, and non-confrontational.

Consistency in the depressed student's life must be the driving force. The adults in his or her life need to apply consistent methods of guidance and expectations of behavior. These children can become very manipulative if they sense inconsistencies in adults. Remain united and consistent when dispensing expectations and consequences. The depressed student gives up very easily and often becomes quickly frustrated. Remain as calm as possible when the student is frustrated or intensely emotional. Be patient, speak softly, and be encouraging in your nonverbal and verbal communication.

Community service, organizations, clubs, and sports that promote healthy activities for adolescents may make depressed students feel they are an important part of the school and community. This will have positive ramifications in the classroom. They will build friendships, have positive interactions, and learn a variety of skills that they can transfer and apply to their schoolwork. Events and activities that involve students and their parents may also help in achieving success in the academic work. Having the parent come to school sometimes motivates the child to show off and, therefore, shine in terms of his or her work. Portfolios are a great way for students to showcase their abilities. The portfolios are multidimensional and may highlight many aspects of the whole child. The student then realizes that there are many skills at which he or she can show proficiency.

This is only a short list of strategies that can be used to facilitate learning for a depressed child. There is great importance in what kind of relationship the child has with his or her teacher, and how that adult is perceived by the student. If the child perceives the adult as caring, supportive, and understanding of their depression, they are more likely to want to please. If the opposite is true, they will become disengaged, defiant, and confrontational. The level of the relationship will have direct impact on the amount and type of work completed. If the child has a sense of mastery and accomplishment, no matter how small the gain, the more likely he or she will persevere. If learned helplessness or a sense of failure has entered the picture, the teacher must do many things over time to rebuild this sense of competency. Low self-esteem will cause many depressed children to be nonproductive and non-participatory in the classroom.

In order to bolster the depressed child's success at school, educators must adapt an environment in which the student can feel safe, supported, and allowed to learn at a slower pace, with less restrictions and rules. In so doing, the educator provides the opportunity for the child to learn at his or her rate while also trying to manage the depression.

Chapter Thirteen

Relationship of Depression to Other Disorders

One of the most well-documented facts about depressive moods, syndromes, and disorders is that they often occur with other symptoms and disorders. Separation anxiety disorder, adjustment disorder with depressed mood, and uncomplicated bereavement are conditions associated with depressive symptoms such as sadness and loss of interest in usual activities. The co-occurrence of disorders is similar for boys and girls, except that boys are more likely to have both disruptive disorders and depression, whereas girls are more likely to have more internalizing behaviors and depression.

Depressive disorders in young people show themselves in different ways, and tend to affect all areas of their lives. Depressed children and adolescents often find school very difficult and are, therefore, reluctant to attend. They often suffer anxiety that may manifest itself in psychosomatic complaints and, thus, poor attendance. Missed school then leads to other issues around failure and acquiring the academic knowledge necessary to be successful. Other depressed young people attend school, but their academic work deteriorates because of problems with concentration and self-organization. They may lose interest and stop caring about being successful. One of the keys to helping these children is communication between home and school.

Sleep problems are common in depressed young people, who often take hours to get to sleep or awake frequently. Such difficulties are common where there is no routine to the child's day, or where he or she may sleep late and not be able to get to sleep at the regular bedtime. The key is to maintain a set bedtime routine to prevent the awake-all-night/asleep-all-day pattern. At times, sleep-aid medication may be prescribed by a physician, but this method is not highly encouraged with young children. This may lead to a dependence on medication and the child will be unable to develop healthy sleep patterns.

Anger and aggression are often the most prominent symptoms of depression. Usually, the aggression is verbal and often is in response to an adult command or request. Physical aggression including damaging furniture, breaking windows, or destroying household items should not be tolerated, even if the young person is depressed. Accountability for one's action needs to be in effect. Serious physical violence toward family members is rare but not unforeseen. This is more likely if the child has severe behavioral issues. If safety is an issue, it may be necessary to call the police and press charges when physical violence has gotten out of control. Being depressed does not justify causing injury.

There is a link between depression and bullying. It is believed that the bullying may be a major factor in maintaining and enhancing the level of depression experienced. Many depressed children and adolescents are often on the periphery in school, are somewhat withdrawn, and lack close friendships.

The type of bullying at the adolescent level is often more psychological and more difficult to pinpoint or identify. Being deliberately excluded from activities planned by friends, receiving cruel, insulting text messages, or having untrue stories or gossip spread through instant messaging may create an environment rich for adolescent depression. Many children and adolescents find it difficult to admit that they are being bullied. There is a mixture of shame and guilt, and a fear that bringing the bullying to attention will make things worse. It is important to be sensitive to these fears. Subtle psychological bullying is very difficult to identify; however, teachers and parents can watch for subtle changes in the way their child or adolescent is responding to various situations. Many schools now have zero-tolerance policies for bullying behaviors and have specific programs in place to help children work through the issues surrounding bullying.

Obsessive-compulsive disorder is an illness that traps people in seemingly endless cycles of repetitive thoughts that will not leave their minds (obsessions) and in feelings that they must repeat certain actions repeatedly (compulsions). Some children and adolescents with obsessive-compulsive disorder (about 20 percent) have only obsessions or only compulsions; most (about 80 percent) have both. OCD affects adults, teenagers, and small children. It is found in people of all social and economic levels. OCD usually manifests itself before the age of 25; less than 15 percent of people develop the disorder after age 35. About half of all people with OCD experienced onset of the disorder before age 19, and some had symptoms as early as in preschool years. When it begins early in childhood, OCD seems to affect boys more often than girls. In children, the onset of OCD can usually be linked to a stressful event. The obsessions and compulsions in children are similar to those seen in adults. OCD that appears in teenagers usually affects boys and girls equally.

OCD often overlaps with other conditions that may also disrupt a child's or adolescent's life. Young people who have OCD seem to be prone to anxiety disorders such as panic, fears, and phobias. Depression is common in children with OCD. Usually children and adolescents become depressed as a result of the toll OCD takes on their lives, but it is not always clear which comes first. About 70 percent of people who have OCD report having had depressive episodes as well. Adolescents with OCD may compound their difficulty by turning to alcohol and drug use to escape the distress of their depression and OCD.

Few illnesses have undergone such an amazing turn of events as OCD. Long suffered in silence, OCD has emerged as a surprisingly common disorder that may respond to drug and behavior therapy. There is still much to learn about the connection between depression and OCD. Through the efforts of researchers, physicians, patients, families, and schools, the lives of these children and adolescents have already been improved and continue to get better.

Attention deficit hyperactivity disorder (ADHD) is a condition that becomes apparent in some children in the preschool and early school years. It is difficult for these children to control their behavior and/or pay attention. It is estimated that between three percent and five percent of children have ADHD, or approximately two million children in the United States. The principal characteristics of ADHD are inattention, hyperactivity, and impulsivity. Symptoms will appear over the course of many months. Different symptoms may appear in different settings, depending upon the demands the situation may pose for the child's self-control. A child with ADHD faces a difficult but not insurmountable task. In order to achieve his or her full potential, he or she should receive help, guidance, and support from the adults and organizations around them.

There is little evidence at this time that ADHD can manifest purely from social factors or child-rearing methods. Most of the substantiated causes appear to fall into the realm of neurobiology and genetics. This is not to say that environmental factors may not influence the severity of the disorder, and especially the degree of impairment and suffering the child may experience. However, such factors alone do not seem to give rise to the conditions.

Some children with ADHD often have co-occurring anxiety or depression. If the anxiety or depression is recognized and treated, the child will be better able to cope with the problems that accompany ADHD. Conversely, effective treatment of ADHD can have a positive effect on anxiety, as the child is better able to master tasks at school and at home. There are no accurate statistics on how many children with ADHD also have bipolar disorder. Differentiating between ADHD and bipolar disorder in childhood can be difficult. In its classic form, bipolar disorder is characterized by moods cycling between periods of intense highs and lows. In children, bipolar disorder often seems to be a rather chronic mood disregulation with a mixture of elation, depression, and irritability. Furthermore, some symptoms may be present in ADHD and bipolar disorder, including high level of energy and a reduced need for sleep. Of the symptoms differentiating children with ADHD from those with bipolar disorder, elated mood and grandiosity of the bipolar child are distinguishing characteristics. Since a child with bipolar disorder will probably be prescribed a mood stabilizer, the physician will carefully consider whether the child should take one of the medications usually prescribed for ADHD. If a stimulant medication is prescribed, it may be given in a lower dosage than usual.

Several intervention approaches are available for ADHD. Psychotherapy works to help children with ADHD to like and accept themselves despite their disorder. It does not address the symptoms or underlying causes of the disorder. Behavior therapy helps children develop more effective ways to work on immediate issues. Rather than helping the child understand his or her feelings and actions, it helps directly in changing their thinking and coping and, thus, may lead to changes in behavior. Social-skills training may also help children learn new behaviors. In this training the child learns new models for appropriate behaviors in developing and maintaining social relationships. Social-skills training may also help the child to develop better ways to play and work with other children, while parent-skills training may give parents tools and techniques for managing their child's behavior and affect. Parents may learn to structure situations in ways that will allow their child to succeed. They may also learn to use stress-management methods, such as mediation, relaxation techniques, and exercise to increase their own tolerance for frustration, in order to respond more calmly to their child's behavior.

Post-traumatic stress disorder (PTSD) may co-exist with depression. Children and adolescents may develop PTSD after living through a terrible and scary experience. Children and adolescents who experience PTSD may have been raped or sexually abused, hit or harmed by someone in the family, been a victim of a violent crime, survived an airplane or car crash, hurricane, tornado, fire, war, or an event in which they thought they may be killed. Symptoms may also develop after observing any of these events. Children with PTSD often experience nightmares and scary thoughts, and regress back to earlier developmental stages. These children often feel angry and are unable to trust other people, and are always on the lookout for dangers. The child becomes easily upset when something happens without warning.

For most children, the PTSD starts within three months of the event. For others, signs do not appear for years. PTSD can manifest itself in anyone. The scary memories lead to depression, trouble sleeping, or anger. These problems keep the child or adolescent from doing everyday things and enjoying life. The important point is that PTSD may hide the depression, and vice versa. It can be treated with medications and therapy. There is hope with the right diagnosis and treatment.

Eating disorders involve serious disturbances in eating behavior, such as extreme and unhealthy reduction of food intake or severe overeating, as well as feelings of distress or extreme concern about body shape or weight. Eating disorders are not due to a failure of will or behavior; rather, they are real, treatable medical illnesses in which certain maladaptive patterns of eating take on a life of their own. The main types of eating disorders are anorexia nervosa, bulimia nervosa, and binge-eating disorder. Onset is often in adolescence, but may occur during childhood.

Eating disorders frequently occur with other psychiatric disorders such as depression, substance abuse, and anxiety disorders. Females are much more likely than males to develop an eating disorder because they have more of a tendency to internalize their depression, as compared with males who will externalize it with some level of aggression. Eating disorders can be treated and a healthy weight restored. The sooner the diagnosis, the better the treatment results.

Eating disorders require a comprehensive treatment plan involving medical care and monitoring, psychosocial interventions, nutritional counseling and, when appropriate, medication management. Individual psychotherapy (especially cognitive-behavioral or interpersonal psychotherapy), and group psychotherapy have been reported to be effective. Psychotropic medications, primarily antidepressants such as selective serotonin re-uptake inhibitors, may be helpful for people with bulimia, particularly those with significant symptoms of depression or anxiety. Adolescents with eating disorders often do not recognize or admit that they are ill. As a result, they may strongly resist getting and/or continuing treatment. Family members or other trusted individuals can be helpful in ensuring that the adolescent with an eating disorder receives needed care and rehabilitation. For some adolescents, treatment may be long-term or lifelong.

Social phobia, also called social anxiety disorder, involves overwhelming anxiety and excessive self-consciousness in everyday social situations. Children and adolescents with social phobia have a persistent, intense, and chronic fear of being watched, judged by others, and of being embarrassed or humiliated by their own actions. These fears may interfere with school and ordinary life activities. The physical symptoms that often accompany the intense anxiety include blushing, profuse sweating, trembling, nausea, and difficulty talking. This disorder usually begins in childhood or early adolescence, and there is some evidence that genetic factors are involved. It coexists with depression. Substance abuse and drug use are ways in which sufferers self-medicate. This phobia can be treated successfully with carefully targeted psychotherapy or medication. The comorbidity of anxiety disorders with depressive disorders in adolescence is estimated at a low of 30 percent and a high of 70 percent. It is often very difficult to separate the symptoms of anxiety and depression and to determine whether one disorder is primary and the other is secondary.

Refusal to attend school or difficulty attending school for the entire day has perplexed educators. One of the problems in this group is the prevalence of symptoms and syndromes or diagnosis of depression in much of this population. Following a review of major studies that evaluated a diagnostic relationship between depression and school refusal behavior, a significant overlap was found between individual clinical entities, suggesting that depression may be considered a common feature of this population. There is a high degree of phobic anxiety present in this population as well. Many are phobic about school attendance. Depressive symptoms in school refusal behavior are most likely to occur among adolescents.

Many children and adolescents with school refusal behavior disorder were identified as having the following characteristics: (1) general fearfulness and extensiveness of the disorder, (2) mutual separation anxiety, (3) perfectionism and fear of failure, and (4) manipulativeness. One can infer that symptoms of depression are characteristic of the fear of failure and extensive disorder. There is a relationship between symptoms of depression, pervasive fear, separation, and perfectionism in children with school refusal behavior disorder. Many children with school refusal behavior disorder present symptoms of depression that are not identified by traditional methods of classification. It is likely, however, that these concurrent symptoms are crucial to the development of effective, prescriptive treatment plans.

Researchers who consider depression to be primary found that children who were identified as depressed had academic and cognitive scores which would classify them as learning disabled. Several studies have proposed that depression results from a diagnosis of a learning disability. Studies of children identified as learning disabled found that the students evidenced a higher rate of depressive symptoms than did non-learning disabled peers. Recognizing depressive symptoms in children with learning disabilities may be difficult for parents and teachers, given the common characteristics between depression and learning disability, such as hyperactivity, conduct disorder, aggression, suicidal ideation, peer rejection, and withdrawal. A suggestion is to obtain an early assessment of skill deficit and program. This would be accomplished through effective programming with proper accommodations and modifications in curriculum presentation and mastery of required skill at that particular level. Schools can be instrumental in developing appropriate and effective programs for learning disabled children regardless if the child is depressed.

A child or adolescent who has a conduct disorder exhibits a persistent pattern of antisocial behavior that significantly impairs everyday functioning at home or school or leads others to conclude that the child is unmanageable. Conduct disorder encompasses a broad range of antisocial behavior such as aggressive acts, theft, vandalism, setting fires, lying, truancy, and running away. Although these behaviors are diverse; their common characteristic is that they tend to violate major social rules and expectations. Many of the behaviors often reflect action against the environment, including persons and property.

The overlap between conduct disorder and depression is estimated anywhere between 20 percent and 35 percent in adolescents and children. Many studies have strongly identified a consistent relationship between social competence deficits and depression and conduct problems. It has also been suggested that anger is common to depression and conduct disorders. It may be that anger is a critical dimension that results in the association of social competence to conduct problems and depression. There is a tendency for these children to have difficulties establishing relationships and, when they do, children tend to act aggressively and inappropriately within them. Although anger is characteristic of some conduct-problem children and some depressed children, it may not be relevant to self-perception or actual social competence.

Depression silently intrudes into children's lives. It is so widespread and easily camouflaged that educators and parents are having a very difficult time even acknowledging the vastness and frequency of the problem. When manifested by itself, depression can be identified, addressed, and undergo specific interventions for its control and remediation. It becomes a challenge to all when the depression is part of a web of dysfunctional behaviors and actions.

At times, the depression is overshadowed by the other existing conditions that make it very difficult to arrive at the true cause or root of the problems the child is experiencing. One failsafe strategy is to ensure extensive assessment and observations to be able to identify the thread that runs through the symptoms and can help parents and educators make associations and connections. Treatment can only be effective if the issue or disorder is identified correctly. There must to be confidence in the diagnosis, leading to improvement or cure rather than finding temporary solutions that will not be effective long-term.

Chapter Fourteen

Self-Help Measures for Depressed Students

Avoiding depression and staying well requires a concentrated effort on the part of the individual and the people around him or her. It is not easy to begin living life fully when one has no motivation to do so, or no obvious reason to get out of bed and participate fully in life. Parents may play a role in their child's ability to self-help with how they express their viewpoints on depression. If a parent is a major player in the child's life, the child is more likely to respond in positive ways toward helping themselves become part of the family unit or in the classroom.

How can a parent or teacher help a child stay well? First, a child on medications must be monitored by the adult, but also by the child. Self-management strategies need to be taught for thc administration and daily regimen of taking the medication. It has to be emphasized frequently that not taking the medication regularly leads to side effects that impede the recovery or maintenance of the program to regulate the depression.

It is important to remind the child that taking the medication will not lead to an instant cure; it may take a while before the child begins to feel better. It is imperative that the child be taught how to recognize how his or her body is reacting to the medications. How does she or he feel at certain times of the day? After taking the medications? Does it affect his or her sleep? Is he or she seeing an improvement? Help the child to self-monitor and keep a running record of good or bad days. This will help the physicians to track the efficiency of the medication.

It is highly encouraged that the child be taught how to recognize his or her own responses and feelings and compare that with some of the actions and behaviors that are happening daily or weekly. This will help the child find out what the illness makes him or her say or do or think. This record keeping can occur verbally and in written form. The child needs to be encouraged to tell his or her parents when these things come and go as well as what the response is on the part of the child.

One thing that has helped many children to self-monitor is the use of art and writing. Younger children can be given supplies to express their emotion in the form of drawings and paintings. Helping the child channel his or her frustration, depression, or even anger into an art form can be very telling about what is occurring internally for the child. Creative writing, poetry, short stories, and other forms of writing can also help older children and adolescents funnel their emotions into creative aspects. Often the characters within the writing are reflections of themselves and the agony or depression that they are feeling at the moment. The use of art can be a wonderful avenue toward inner discovery and dialogue.

Support groups for children with depression can accomplish at least two things. They can normalize the children's experience, or help them become more dramatic and dysfunctional based on the behaviors they observe. The type of support group a child enters is paramount to the function of the participation in the group and reasons why the child is there in the first place. If the reason for the group is to build involvement in social activities, it has to be regulated and watched closely so that the child does not become isolated within that environment. Parents often think that if their child is around other children, he or she will participate. This is often not the case. The reverse often occurs, with the child withdrawing even more into isolation and depression.

One of the causes of depression for children stems from what happens in their daily life and how those events lead to functional or dysfunctional living. Creating an open door of communication about school is an avenue by which a child can feel free to express and discuss any fears or concerns that may arise. Often anxieties become great fuel for the depression. Helping the child discuss any of these concerns in an open way will help the adult process the information with the child in a way that the child can make sense of or comprehend the true factors at play.

Physical well-being can be improved with taking a walk, riding a bicycle, going swimming, and many other activities. Do not force a child to take part in physical activities he or she despises. This will only create more stress and, therefore, more likelihood that the depression will be accentuated when the child feels that he or she is incompetent or cannot meet expectations. Physical well-being also includes eating healthy food and getting plenty of rest and relaxation as well. Food intake should be monitored to assure proper nutrition and a well-balanced daily regimen.

Several skills may be taught so that the child can become more empowered to control or regulate his or her depression. The first skill is the ability to recognize and tolerate ambiguity. The child needs to understand that in many situations there is no single correct answer, but rather several possibilities. For many depressed children, this ambiguity leads to stress and insecurity, which in turn leads to making the wrong choices and, therefore, leading to the likelihood that they will make negative interpretations of the situation, thus reinforcing their depression.

The second skill is to teach critical thinking to the child or adolescent. Critical thinking helps children understand and discriminate between things for which they are responsible and the things for which they are not. Teaching children to understand the level of control and to evaluate that amount will often lead to a sense of ability rather than a sense of inability. If children assume that they are helpless when they are not, they do not even try.

Another factor that influences the amount of guilt a child may have regards responsibilities and the accomplishment of those responsibilities. If children have the perspective of not being able to meet the standards as set by the adult in their lives, they are more likely to feel like failures and become even more depressed. One solution is to help children discriminate between ways in which they are defined by their achievements and ways in which they are not. It is important to help children realize when it is acceptable to focus on the present and when it is better to focus on the future.

The third skill that helps children with self-care is the ability to clearly articulate goals. First, they must be the goals of the child, and not those of the adults. They need to be child-generated and the timeline needs to be developed with the child and adult in collaboration. Creating a flowchart or a visual that can be posted will serve as a reminder for the child, while keeping the family on the right path. It is better to set realistic and attainable goals that can be accomplished quickly and frequently with some long-term goals to encourage future planning.

The fourth skill is learning to discriminate between what the child is feeling versus what is objectively true. It is crucial to help the child to understand what is happening inside their head and what is truly happening in their environments, and also how those may be different. Helping to clarify the differences helps the child stay in reality. It also helps the child to be able to monitor when they are slipping into their unhealthy thinking or beliefs.

The fifth skill is to ensure that the child develops and maintains relationships, since relationships act as buffers against illness and emotional disorders. A child who is most at risk for depression is a lonely child. Children want to be included in groups, families, and society. Teaching the child healthy boundaries, the rules of certain types of relationships, and giving specific teaching or advice will enable the child to become more likely to be involved with the people around him or her.

In helping depressed children and adolescents help themselves, one must teach them a new vocabulary of thinking. The Pain to Power Vocabulary is used in creating new beliefs in the child. Many students see themselves as either victims or helpless, so giving them some new ways of channeling their thinking about life, situations, and themselves is empowering. The words "I can't" are based in pain because they signify a sense of helplessness. Therefore, it is necessary to change them to words of power, such as "I won't." Help the child see that "I won't" allows for the ability to choose and make decisions about whether something is done or not done.

The words "I should" are full of expectations and, therefore, add more pressure and responsibility. The power vocabulary is "I would," which allows the individual the choice to decide whether it is a good time to do something, it is convenient, or if the person has the desire to accomplish it.

The pain words of "It is not my fault" signify abdication of responsibility for an action, or the fact that the situation is to be blamed on someone else. The power vocabulary is, "I am totally responsible." This belief encourages accountability and helps the individuals become more assertive in the choices they make. They are influencing their destinies.

The pain words "It is a problem," which indicate lack of ability to solve and/or resolve an issue, are changed to power words: "It is an opportunity." Seeing a problem as an opportunity helps an individual tap into his or her creativity or resourcefulness to solve and take advantage of a situation rather than feeling like a victim and unable to act.

The pain words "I am never satisfied," which reinforce the thoughts of never being happy or never getting what one needs or wants, are changed to a power statement: "I want to learn to grow." This switch in perspective helps the child understand that new experiences are not meant to be feared, but to be experienced and lived. This helps the child experiment with new events and new situations.

The pain words "Life is a struggle" become "Life is an adventure," creating an environment for excitement and new experiences as compared with leading a sedate, exiled existence. Once the child sees that life may be tough at times, it can also be exciting and a wonderful journey of discovery. There needs to be a sense of anticipation for what is just around the corner. Children, especially the youngest still experience the wow factor. They can be impressed with many new things.

Reversing the pain words of "I hope" to the power words of "I know" establishes a sense of security and definition. It provides the individuals with the ability to recognize what they do know and what they can do about a situation or person. They are aware of what skills are necessary and are more in control of what the possible results of the interaction may be. There is more predictability for the outcomes.

The pain words "What will I do?" are changed to the power words of "I know I can handle it," indicating an ability to let less happen by chance and to be more in control of the situation. Children move from a place of having to wait for someone to tell them what to do to deciding what is in their best interests or aligns with one of their goals and, therefore, needs to be done to achieve that goal.

Turning "It is terrible" into "It is a learning experience" helps put a situation into a perspective that leads to a better comprehension of the event, what can be done, and how the learning can be used as future reference for other upcoming events or crises.

Teaching the child or adolescent to recognize the pain vocabulary and how it influences and determines the path of depression is paramount in helping him or her recognize how these thoughts are influencing his or her actions. Providing the child with the power vocabulary and how to counteract the negativity of the pain vocabulary helps him or her to feel more self-aware, empowered, in control, and en route to recovery. Changing adolescents' vocabulary is tough and will only occur if it is done systemically and reinforced positively every time it is demonstrated. The individual needs to see specific evidence of how the power vocabulary influenced his or her actions and how the results of those actions are linked to the way the individual frames it in his or her thinking processes.

Helping depressed children take care of themselves during this period of depression may often be the catalyst between them feeling totally vulnerable and victimized by their circumstances to feeling empowered and able to manage the complexities of their depression. It is imperative that the adults in a depressed child's life act as models to reinforce the positive thinking aspects of the power vocabulary. These adults can demonstrate, encourage, and guide the child or adolescent through some of the struggles of learning new ways of thinking and doing. Providing very specific guidance in a loving and compassionate way will help the child or adolescent build a sense of self-esteem and confidence in himself or herself and influence his or her choices and actions.

Chapter Fifteen

Medications and Therapies

Childhood is supposed to be a time of joy, learning, and growth. However, a child hampered by learning disabilities, antisocial behavior, or severe depression is robbed of one of the most precious periods of life. Mental-health advocates, employing a very broad and inclusive definition, now estimate that almost 21 percent of U.S. children between the ages of 9 and 17 have some sort of "diagnosable" mental or addictive disorder associated with at least minimum impairment. No matter how it is defined, the problem does seem to be growing worse. The suicide rate among 15- to 24-year-olds has tripled since 1960. Suicide is now the third leading cause of death in this age group, and the sixth leading cause among children aged 5 to 15.

Between 200,000 and 300,000 children suffer from autism, a developmental disorder that prevents learning and other cognitive growth. Three to five percent of all children have attention deficit hyperactivity disorder (ADHD), also known among others as minimal brain dysfunction. These children cannot concentrate, learn, or behave "normally." They cannot finish a project, do not seem to listen, and require very close supervision. They can be very bright, yet unable to focus their intelligence. Tragically, many are labeled "troublemakers" and shunted aside in schools and homes that do not understand the problem.

Conduct disorder, or CD, afflicts more adolescent boys and girls than any other emotional illness. As many as nine percent of males and two percent of females are in the grip of violent, socially unacceptable behavior patterns that lead them to destroy property, steal, and make physical or sexual attacks on others. CD may arise from a combination of biological predisposition and environmental influence that is not fully understood. Whatever the cause, CD refers to a specific set of behaviors, not merely to a difficult teenager who is moody and hard to control. Children also suffer from several forms of anxiety similar to those seen in adults. For example, separation anxiety can lead a child to consistently refuse to leave a parent's side. It may be more apparent when the school years begin, but may strike at any time.

Phobias, too, are common among children. They include fear of the dark, animals, and certain colors. In fact, according to some estimates, as many as 43 percent of children under age 12 have some sort of exaggerated fear. Curbing mental illness in children is often controversial, since children are harder to treat effectively on an outpatient basis than are adults. Often their problems stem from sexual or physical abuse, drug addiction, genetic conditions, or dysfunctional family environments. If a child is left in the same destructive environment that caused the problem, medication or therapy may not be effective solutions.

Treatment for children almost always includes the entire family. For some problems, such as depression, anxiety, and phobias, the same medications used in adults can, with close supervision by a doctor, be effective in conjunction with family therapy. Treatment for ADHD involves medications such as Ritalin, Focalin, Desoxyn, Adderall, Cylert, Concerta, Metadate, Methylin, and Dexedrine; and a special educational track that enables the student to remain in school with his peers and family therapy. Medications enable the child to control his impulsive behavior and perform without loss of attention. The American Psychiatric Association reports that between 70 and 80 percent of ADHD patients "respond to medications when they are properly used." Children with conduct disorders must have treatment that includes behavioral therapy and, when appropriate, medications for underlying depression or ADHD, if present. Many people define mental illness as "the absence of mental health." After all, we all know when we do or do not "feel good," mentally and physically. However, as you can see by the variety of disorders, this definition is simplistic. A mental illness is a specific problem that causes a sustained disruption of your general well-being, behavior, or mood, and interferes with your normal functioning. It can result in *either* psychological or physiological symptoms. The most important things to remember about mental illness are that it can usually be treated effectively, that it is not a sign of weakness or failure, that it is nobody's fault, and that getting help as soon as possible is a vital part of treatment.

In the following pages is a list of a variety of medications and some of their side effects (from the *PDR Family Guide to Prescription Drugs*). The discussion is based on what the drug is used for. This list is not exhaustive and some of the medications may be used under other names. Consultation with your physician is highly recommended before beginning any type of treatment using medications.

PSYCHOSTIMULANTS AND SEDATIVES

Desoxyn

Desoxyn (generic name: methamphetamine hydrochloride) is used to treat ADHD. Side effects cannot be anticipated. If any develop or change in intensity, inform your doctor as soon as possible. Only your doctor can determine if it is safe to continue taking Desoxyn. Side effects may include: changes in sex drive, constipation, diarrhea, dizziness, dry mouth, exaggerated feeling of well-being, headache, hives, impaired growth, impotence, increased blood pressure, overstimulation, rapid or irregular heartbeat, restlessness, sleeplessness, stomach or intestinal problems, tremor, unpleasant taste, worsening of tics, and Tourette's syndrome (severe twitching).

Adderall

Adderall is prescribed in the treatment of ADHD, the condition in which a child exhibits a short attention span and becomes easily distracted, overly emotional, excessively active, and highly impulsive. It should be used as part of a broader treatment plan that includes psychological, educational, and social measures. An extended-release form of the drug, called Adderall XR, is available for once-daily treatment of ADHD. Side effects of Adderall may include: dry mouth, high blood pressure, hives, impotence, overstimulation, rapid or pounding heartbeat, stomach and intestinal disturbances, and weight loss.

Dexedrine

Dexedrine, a stimulant drug available in tablet or sustained-release capsule form, is prescribed to help treat the following conditions: Narcolepsy (recurrent "sleep attacks") and ADHD. (The total treatment program should include social, psychological, and educational guidance along with Dexedrine.) Side effects may include: excessive restlessness and overstimulation. Effects of chronic heavy abuse of Dexedrine may include: hyperactivity, irritability, personality changes, schizophrenia-like thoughts and behavior, severe insomnia, and serious skin disease. Narcolepsy seldom occurs in children under 12 years of age; however, when it does, Dexedrine may be used. The suggested initial dose for children between 6 and 12 years of age is five milligrams per day. Your doctor may increase the daily dose in increments of five milligrams at weekly intervals until it becomes effective. Children 12 years of age and older will be started with 10 milligrams daily. The daily dosage may be raised in increments of 10 milligrams at weekly intervals until effective. If side effects such as insomnia or loss of appetite appear, the dosage will probably be reduced. This drug is not recommended for children under three years of age. Children from three to five years of age are usually prescribed 2.5 milligrams daily in tablet form. A physician may raise the daily dosage by 2.5 milligrams at weekly intervals until the drug takes effect. Children six years and older start at a dose of five milligrams once or twice a day, and the dose may be raised by five milligrams at weekly intervals until satisfied with the response. Only in rare cases will the child take more than 40 milligrams a day. Your child should take the first dose when he or she wakes up; the remaining one or two doses are taken at intervals of every four to six hours. Alternatively, a physician may prescribe "Spansule" capsules that are taken once a day. A physician may interrupt the schedule occasionally to see if behavioral symptoms come back enough to require continued therapy.

Deanol

Deanol or dimethylaminoethanol is presently marketed as a dietary supplement, but at one time it was used as a drug for the treatment of hyperactivity in children. It was also used for such conditions as neuroleptic-induced tardive dyskinesia. Deanol was thought to affect tardive dyskinesia because it was believed to be a cholinergic precursor and to enhance acetylcholine synthesis in the brain. It is now known that, although Deanol is a precursor to choline, very little of the choline formed from it is converted to acetylcholine in the brain.

Ritalin

Ritalin and other brands of methylphenidate are mild central nervous system stimulants used in the treatment of ADHD in children. When given for attention deficit disorder, Ritalin should be an integral part of a total treatment program that includes psychological, educational, and social measures. Symptoms of attention deficit disorder include continual problems with moderate to severe distractibility, short attention span, hyperactivity, emotional changeability, and impulsiveness. This drug should not be given to children under six years of age. Side effects cannot be anticipated. If any develop or change in intensity, inform a physician as soon as possible. He or she can determine if it is safe to continue giving Ritalin. Side effects may include inability to fall or stay asleep, and nervousness.

SEDATIVES AND HYPNOTICS

Elavil

Elavil is prescribed for the relief of symptoms of mental depression. It is a member of the group of drugs called tricyclic antidepressants. Some doctors also prescribe Elavil to treat the eating disorder bulimia, control chronic pain, prevent migraine headaches, and to treat a pathological weeping and laughing syndrome associated with multiple sclerosis. Use of Elavil is not recommended for children under 12 years of age. The usual dose for adolescents 12 years and older is 10 milligrams, three times a day, with 20 milligrams taken at bedtime. Side effects may include: blurred vision, bone marrow depression, bowel problems, breast enlargement (in males and females), constipation, dry mouth, hair loss, heart attack, high body temperature, problems urinating, rash, seizure, stroke, swelling of the testicles, and water retention.

Side effects due to a rapid decrease in dose or abrupt withdrawal from Elavil include: headache, nausea, and vague feeling of bodily discomfort. Side effects due to gradual dosage reduction may include: dream and sleep disturbances, irritability, and restlessness.

Restoril

Restoril is used for the relief of insomnia (difficulty in falling asleep, waking frequently at night, or waking early in the morning). It belongs to a class of drugs known as benzodiazepines. The safety and effectiveness of Restoril have not been established in children younger than 18.

Phenobarbital

Phenobarbital, a barbiturate, is used as a sleep aid and in the treatment of certain types of epilepsy, including generalized or grand mal seizures and partial seizures. Side effects may include: allergic reaction, drowsiness, headache, lethargy, nausea, oversedation, sleepiness, slowed or delayed breathing, vertigo, and vomiting.

ANTIPSYCHOTIC MEDICATIONS

Clozaril

Clozaril is given to help people with severe schizophrenia who have failed to respond to standard treatments. It is also used to help reduce the risk of suicidal behavior in people with schizophrenia. Clozaril is not a cure, but it can help some people return to more normal lives. Safety and efficacy have not been established for children up to 16 years of age. Some side effects include: abdominal discomfort, agitation, blood disorders, confusion, constipation, disturbed sleep, dizziness, drowsiness, dry mouth, fainting, fever, headache, heartburn, high blood pressure, inability to sit down, loss or slowness of muscle movement, low blood pressure, nausea, nightmares, rapid heartbeat and other heart conditions, restlessness, rigidity, salivation, sedation, sweating, tremors, vertigo, vision problems, vomiting, and weight gain.

Prochlorperazine

Prochlorperazine is used to control severe nausea and vomiting. It is also used to treat symptoms of schizophrenia, and is occasionally prescribed for anxiety. Side effects may include: blurred vision, dizziness, drowsiness, jaundice, low blood pressure, menstrual irregularities, neuroleptic malignant syndrome, and skin reactions.

ANTIDEPRESSANTS

Depression can take hold as a result of a serious illness or loss, but it can also appear without any apparent cause. It is a condition that affects the entire individual, including the mind, mood, and body. It can cause tremendous anguish for the patient and those who care about him or her. One study found that patients with depressive symptoms felt significantly worse and experienced more limitations than patients with hypertension, diabetes, arthritis, or gastrointestinal disorders. Only patients with angina or advanced heart disease had more difficulty with physical functioning, and none had worse social functioning.

Heterocyclic Antidepressants

Heterocyclics prove safe and effective for up to 80 percent of the people who take them. For the first few weeks, some patients experience blurred vision, constipation, a feeling of light-headedness or confusion, dry mouth, weight gain, or retention of urine. A small percentage complained of such other side effects as sweating, racing heartbeat, low blood pressure, or allergic skin reactions. Serious side effects, which are extremely rare, include elevated pressure in the eyes and seizures. Most side effects disappear after a few weeks, when the therapeutic effects of the medication take hold. The medication is beginning to work when insomnia gradually clears up, energy begins to return, self-esteem improves, and feelings of hopelessness, helplessness, and sadness decline. Some of the prominent heterocyclic antidepressants are: Amitriptyline (Elavil, Etrafon, Limbitrol), Desipramine (Norpramin), Doxepin (Sinequan, Adapin), Imipramine (Tofranil), Nortriptyline (Aventyl, Pamelor), Protriptyline (Vivactil), and Trimipramine (Surmontil).

Serotonin Re-Uptake Inhibitors

Prozac is the best known of this class of medication, although several variations are available. These drugs generally have fewer troublesome side effects than other antidepressants. Since these medications have less effect on the cardiovascular system, they are helpful for depressed people who have suffered a stroke or have heart disease. However, side effects occur in some people during the first few days including anxiety, sleep disturbances, stomach cramps, nausea, and skin rash. In extremely rare cases, a person may experience a seizure. Most side effects disappear after a few weeks, although some people report a sustained decrease in sexual function. After one to four weeks, the effects of the medication become apparent, and many people report feeling "like a new person." In general, the drug may be continued as long as necessary to prevent recurrence of depression. There are no known "late" side effects of the drug; some people should take it indefinitely. Serotonin re-uptake inhibitors and similar drugs available include: Citalopram (Celexa), Fluoxetine (Prozac), Nefazodone (Serzone), Paroxetine (Paxil), Sertraline (Zoloft), and Venlafaxine (Effexor).

Monoamine Oxidase Inhibitors (MAO Inhibitors)

Although these drugs are as effective as other classes of antidepressants, they are prescribed less often because of their required dietary restrictions. Patients taking MAO inhibitors must avoid aged cheese, yogurt, liver, certain beans, and large amounts of alcohol, caffeine, or chocolate. Because of the risk of serious interactions, they also must check with a physician before taking any over-the-counter or prescription drugs. MAO inhibitors are usually prescribed when a person has not responded to other antidepressants. They are also useful for depressed people whose health conditions (such as heart ailments or glaucoma) prevent them from taking other types of antidepressants. Monoamine oxidase inhibitors include: Isocarboxazid (Marplan), Phenelzine (Nardil), and Tranylcypromine (Parnate).

Lithium

This drug is the medication of choice for those with bipolar illness. The manic symptoms usually diminish in 5 to 14 days and depressive symptoms are reduced. Side effects include: tremor, weight gain, nausea, mild diarrhea, and skin rashes. People should drink 10 to 12 glasses of water a day to avoid dehydration while on lithium. Less frequently, patients encounter confusion, slurred speech, extreme fatigue, excitement, muscle weakness, dizziness, difficulty in walking, or sleep disturbances. Physicians also may prescribe anticonvulsant drugs such as carbamazepine or valproate. Anticonvulsant drugs have been known to cause serious blood disorders in some.

Haldol

Haldol is used to reduce the symptoms of disorders such as schizophrenia. It is also prescribed to control tics (uncontrolled muscle contractions of face, arms, or shoulders) and the unintended utterances that mark Tourette's syndrome. In addition, it is used in short-term treatment of children with severe behavior problems, including hyperactivity and combativeness. Side effects may include: breast development in men, breathing difficult, cataracts, constipation, drowsiness, dry mouth, insomnia, involuntary muscle contractions, skin reactions, tardive dyskinesia, tightening of the throat muscles, and weight loss.

Mellaril

Mellaril combats schizophrenia (a severe loss of contact with reality). Since Mellaril has been known to cause dangerous heartbeat irregularities, it is usually prescribed only when at least two other medications have failed. The usual starting dose for schizophrenic children is 0.5 milligrams per 2.2 pounds of body weight per day, divided into smaller doses. The dose may be gradually increased to a maximum of three milligrams per 2.2 pounds per day. Side effects may include: blurred vision, breast development in men, breast milk secretion, constipation, diarrhea, drowsiness, dry mouth, impotence, nausea, swelling in the arms and legs (edema), tardive dyskinesia, and vomiting.

Moban

Moban is used in the treatment of schizophrenia. The safety and effectiveness of Moban in children under age 12 have not been established.

Side effects may include: blurred vision, depression, drowsiness (especially at the start of therapy), dry mouth, euphoria, hyperactivity, nausea, Parkinson's-like movements, and restlessness.

Navane

Navane is used in the treatment of schizophrenia. Researchers theorize that antipsychotic medications (such as Navane) work by lowering levels of dopamine, a neurotransmitter (or chemical messenger) in the brain. Excessive levels of dopamine are believed to be related to psychotic behavior. Navane is not recommended for children younger than 12. Side effects may include: agitation, blood disorders, blurred vision, drowsiness, dry mouth, exaggerated reflexes, fainting, high blood pressure, insomnia, light-headedness, low blood pressure, Parkinson's-like movements, profuse sweating, rapid or irregular heartbeat, rash, sensitivity to sunlight, and skin color changes.

Chlorpromazine

Chlorpromazine is used for the treatment of schizophrenia. It is also prescribed for the short-term treatment of severe behavioral disorders in children, including explosive hyperactivity and combativeness, and for the manic phase of bipolar disorder. Chlorpromazine is generally not prescribed for children younger than six months. Side effects may include: constipation, drowsiness, dry mouth, involuntary muscle spasms and twitches (tardive dyskinesia), jaundice, low blood pressure, low white blood cell count, movements similar to Parkinson's disease, neuroleptic malignant syndrome, rapid heartbeat, restlessness, and vision problems.

Medications called "antipsychotics," which include Thorazine, Haldol, Trilafon, Serentil, Moban, Risperdal, and the new schizophrenia drugs Geodon, Seroquel, and Zyprexa, seem to be effective in reducing symptoms in up to 80 percent of all patients. Despite severe side effects such as tardive dyskinesia, which afflicts 20 to 30 percent of patients with involuntary movements of the mouth and tongue, these medications combat the hallucinations and delusions that are the hallmarks of schizophrenia. As these symptoms subside, psychotherapy and group therapy for the family and patient can create an environment in which the patient can function once again.

Triavil

Triavil is used to treat anxiety, agitation, and depression. Triavil is a combination of a tricyclic antidepressant (amitriptyline) and a tranquilizer (perphenazine). Triavil can also help people with schizophrenia who are depressed and those with insomnia, fatigue, loss of interest, loss of appetite, or a slowing of physical and mental reactions. This medication is only for adolescents. Side effects may include: disorientation, dry mouth, high or low blood pressure, nervous system disorders, and sedation.

Trilafon

Trilafon is used to treat schizophrenia and to control severe nausea and vomiting in adults. It is a member of the phenothiazine family of antipsychotic medications, which includes such drugs as Mellaril, Stelazine, and Thorazine. Side effects may include: aching or numbness of the limbs, brain swelling, breast milk production, diarrhea, drowsiness, dry mouth, low blood pressure upon standing, nausea, rapid or irregular heartbeat, restlessness, salivation, seizures, and vomiting.

Adapin

Heterocyclic antidepressants prove safe and effective for up to 80 percent of the people who take them. For the first few weeks, some patients experience blurred vision, constipation, light-headedness or confusion, dry mouth, weight gain, or retention of urine. A small percentage complains of other side effects as sweating, racing heartbeat, low blood pressure, or allergic skin reactions. Serious side effects, which are extremely rare, include elevated pressure in the eyes and seizures. Most side effects disappear after a few weeks when the therapeutic effects of the medication take hold.

Anafranil

Anafranil, a chemical cousin of tricyclic antidepressant medications such as Tofranil and Elavil, is used to treat people who suffer from obsessions and compulsions. An obsession is a persistent and disturbing idea, image, or urge that keeps coming to mind despite the person's efforts to ignore or forget it. For example, there is a preoccupation with avoiding contamination. A compulsion is an irrational action that the person knows is senseless but feels driven to repeat again and again; for example, hand-washing perhaps dozens or even countless times throughout the day. The usual recommended initial dose is 25 milligrams daily divided into smaller doses and taken with meals. Physicians may gradually increase the dose to a maximum of 100 milligrams or three milligrams per 2.2 pounds of body weight per day, whichever is smaller. The maximum dose is 200 milligrams or three milligrams per 2.2 pounds of body weight, whichever is smaller. Once the dose has been determined, the child can take it in a single dose at bedtime. Side effects may include: constipation, dizziness, dry mouth, impotence, increased appetite, increased sweating, indigestion, libido changes, nausea, nervousness, sleepiness, tremor, twitching, visual changes, weight gain, and weight loss.

Desyrel

Desyrel is prescribed for the treatment of depression. Side effects may include: abdominal or stomach disorder, aches or pains in muscles and bones, anger or hostility, blurred vision, brief loss of consciousness, confusion, constipation, decreased appetite, diarrhea, dizziness or light-headedness, drowsiness, dry mouth, excitement, fainting, fast or fluttery heartbeat, fatigue, fluid retention and swelling, headache, inability to fall or stay asleep, low blood pressure, nasal or sinus congestion, nausea, nervousness, nightmares or vivid dreams, tremors, uncoordinated movements, vomiting, and weight gain or weight loss.

Tofranil

Tofranil is a member of the family of drugs called tricyclic antidepressants. Tofranil is also used on a short-term basis, along with behavioral therapies, to treat bed-wetting in children aged six and older. Its effectiveness may decrease with longer use. Some doctors also prescribe Tofranil to treat bulimia, attention deficit disorder in children, obsessive-compulsive disorder, and panic disorder. Tofranil-PM, which is usually taken once daily at bedtime, is approved to treat major depression. Side effects may include: breast development in males, breast enlargement in females, breast milk production, confusion, diarrhea, dry mouth, hallucinations, hives, high blood pressure, low blood pressure upon standing, nausea, numbness, tremors, and vomiting. The most common side effects in children being treated for bedwetting are: nervousness, sleep disorders, stomach and intestinal problems, tiredness, anxiety, constipation, convulsions, emotional instability, and fainting.

Marplan

This medication is used to treat anxiety and depression. MAO inhibitors are often tried when other antidepressants fail. Included in this group are Phenelzine (Nardil), Tranylcypromine (Parnate), and Isocarboxazid (Marplan). MAO inhibitors cause dangerous interactions with a number of foods and need to be taken with caution.

Under no circumstances are any of these medications being recommended by the author. The use of medications in treating depression is a decision that parent, physician, and child may make together.

MODELS OF THERAPIES FOR DEPRESSION IN CHILDREN

Treatment of depression in children requires sensitivity to their developmental levels and stages. All individuals must follow developmental lines and display sensitivity to the complex interplay of biological, psychological, family, and social problems. Treatment of a depressed child may be indicated on the basis of anticipated damage to development and to future function even though the child is not blatantly symptomatic at the time. The withdrawn, under-functioning child may be in more urgent need of treatment than the aggressive child who is more likely to be referred for professional evaluation and care. Either child may be in need of treatment.

When developing a treatment program, the first consideration is whether depressive symptomatology represents a primary condition, or is a byproduct of other behavior problems. For example, youngsters who are hyperactive, aggressive, school phobic, or socially incompetent may experience depressive symptomatology and related dysfunctional cognitions as a result of these problems (Magg, Behrens, & DiGangi, 1991). Intervention strategies generally reflect either behavioral or cognitive behavioral orientations, or in specific cases, a medical orientation. Although techniques based on these models seem promising, only a few studies have investigated their efficacy with children and adolescents. The professional treating a child or adolescent with major depression is left in a bit of quandary. Clearly, this is a disorder with a high rate of recurrence and remarkable morbidity and mortality. As of yet, however, there are no completed, rigorous, controlled studies showing major efficacy of either specific psychotherapeutic techniques or specific pharmacologic intervention for this group. Studies are underway and with hope their results will shed needed light on this area of research.

The following treatment strategies travel a theoretical model of intervention and fall within four groups: social skills, self-control, helplessness, and cognitive strategies. Each one of these models works on specific ideas and their use is a decision made by the therapist and parent together.

Social Skills Strategies

The main strategies include shaping procedures that use adult reinforcement, modeling, or combined modeling and reinforcement procedures. Direct training procedures make use of the child's cognitive and verbal skills. Specific training techniques include instructions, modeling, role-playing, rehearsal, feedback, and self-management techniques. Verbal-cognitive approaches emphasize teaching specific social skills and general problem solving techniques.

Self-Control Strategies

Self-monitoring, self-evaluation, self-reinforcement, and self-instruction would be appropriate for remediating self-control deficits. Intervention should take into account the child's cognitive developmental capacities and require the practitioner to play an active role in effecting the desired change by utilizing action-oriented techniques and concrete tasks.

Helplessness Strategies

These strategies follow an attribution retraining conceptualization in which children are taught to take responsibility for their failures and to attribute success or failure to effort. Adaptive coping responses are substituted for attributions of helplessness.

Cognitive Strategies

Treatment focuses on determining the meaning of the child's nonverbal and verbal communication. Any distorted cognitions the child expresses must be challenged. Bestowing acceptance and affection are important, as is assigning tasks that ensure success experiences. Techniques are designed to help the child identify, reality-test, and modify distorted conceptualization, and dysfunctional attitudes and beliefs.

In determining the choice of strategies (given the range of deficits associated with depression, and their implications for treatment), it is important to determine which factors seem most responsible for the development of this disorder. Attempting to assess a youngster's relative skills in each area is a tedious and exacting process. Nevertheless, to enhance treatment efficacy, intervention techniques should be matched to identified and specific problems.

In this regard, it is suggested that potential intervention strategies be sequenced and then decisions made on which ones to use in which order, depending on the results of assessment information. The importance of eliciting overt behavior change before targeting cognitive factors should be stressed because overt behavior is easier to assess than reports of children's cognitions. In addition, obtaining an accurate sampling of the child's self-reported cognitions is easier once behavior has been modified. As with any aspect of depression in children and adolescents, care must be taken to modify intervention strategies based on the child's developmental stage and level of cognitive affective and behavioral functioning.

Even as treatment of childhood and adolescent depression seems promising, factors external to the child should be considered. Because of the parents' influence over their children, family-based interventions should be incorporated into treatment programs. Teachers can play a pivotal role by cultivating positive relationships with parents. Positive parent-teacher relationships promote parental feedback to practitioners, enhance treatment outcomes, and extend positive effects of school programming into the home.

In addition, parents can become trainers of their children by structuring activities and managing behavioral contingencies that promote participation in activities and social interactions. Parents have effectively implemented reinforcement and taught pro-social behaviors to their children. Parent programs have resulted in decreases in maternal depression and increased family cohesion.

School-based interventions add several other dimensions as well. Many special educators already conduct social skills training and utilize other cognitive behavioral techniques for working with aggressive and socially incompetent youngsters. Treating depression represents a natural extension of these responsibilities. Furthermore, peers can be recruited for the intervention process as they represent a resource for promoting entrapment of behaviors that may combat depression. Special educators, therefore, may play a vital role in the early identification, assessment, and treatment of depression.

To treat depressed students, one must understand their attempts to alleviate negative internal feelings of unworthiness by soliciting or demanding support and praise from others. A factor to consider is that some depressed students are not aware they are depressed. In these instances, it can be very therapeutic to suggest that such symptoms as constant fatigue, loss of energy, loss of interest in activities, feeling down or sad may be depression.

A critical factor in the treatment of depression is anger. A depressed individual feels guilty about and cannot express angry feelings directly at the object, person, or situation causing the frustration or deprivation. The depressed child experiences the "bad me" role for having such feelings and turns the anger inward as a form of self-punishment. If one could express anger, one would not become depressed.

In particular, the effectiveness of various treatments for depression in children is an area in need of further study and research. Educators are in a relatively unique position for the identification of depression in children and adolescents. Given the number of children suggested by research to be experiencing clinical levels of depression, active procedures need to be implemented in schools for the identification and treatment of these children and adolescents. Likewise, a concurrent focus on suicidal youths should also be considered, given the seriousness and problematic nature of this problem. If educators do not become advocates for the mental health and well-being of children and adolescents, it will be the children who suffer the consequences.

To effectively treat childhood depression, school personnel must become more knowledgeable about this condition, including its forms, precipitating events, characteristics, early detection, and general as well as symptom specific treatment interventions. Early detection and treatment of depressed children before the depression becomes a way of life is essential. The intensity of treatment will depend upon the severity of the child's illness and the degree of the family's psychological health. Given timely and appropriate help, most depressed children and adolescents can be helped to live a normal and productive life.

Chapter Sixteen

Online Depression, Warning Signs, and Interventions

The increasing amount of time children are spending on computers at home and at school has raised questions about how the use of computer technology may make a difference in their lives, from helping with homework, to causing depression, to encouraging violent behaviors. The increased time in front of the computer has also led to obesity rates climbing in children and adolescents. Although evidence in numerous studies have resulted in mixed findings, the effects on social development have been documented. The moderate use of computers to play games has a negative effect on children's friendships and family relationships. Recent survey data show that increased use of the Internet may be linked to increases in loneliness and depression. Of the most concern are the findings that playing violent computer games may increase aggressiveness and desensitize a child to suffering, and that the use of computers may blur a child's ability to distinguish real life from simulation.

When children use computers instead of participating in sports and social activities, it raises concerns about the possible effects on their physical and psychological well-being. Several studies suggest that children's extended computer use may be linked to an increased risk of obesity, seizures, and hand injuries.

The use of home computers not only can influence children's cognitive and academic skills, but can also shape children's social interactions and development. With respect to interactions with peers, the effects of the computer use again appear to depend as much on the type of activity engaged in while on the computer as on the amount of time spent in front of the screen. Because of the importance of interacting with others to gain social competence, children who form electronic friendships with computers instead of friendships with their peers might be hindered in developing their interpersonal skills. The fact that so many children and adolescents are alone in their rooms on a computer, in total isolation, robs them of time for other social activities in which they could be developing and nurturing relationships. Depressed children and adolescents can be sequestered in their rooms without much human interaction.

The more the adolescent or child uses the computer, the less social involvement there is with family and a social network. Using the Internet in itself causes the decline in social well-being. The studies researched were unclear, however, as to whether these effects were because the time spent using the Internet was substituting for time previously spent engaged in social activities, or because social relationships created online provided less social support than those grounded in the offline world.

Social psychologists have long explored the linking of communication, social resources, and psychological well-being. People with greater involvement and support systems, including social and network resources, tend to fair better in their personal lives. People with extraverted individual orientations are likely to have better psychological functioning, lower levels of stress, and greater happiness, thus having less depressive symptoms. By contrast, those with fewer social resources, social isolation, living alone, the absence or breakdown of a close relationship, and low levels of social support and introversion, are more likely to feel lonely and to experience high levels of depressive affect.

Scholars have offered alternative arguments about the effects of Internet use on people's social resources, with different implications for changes in the well-being of Internet users. The social augmentation hypothesis is that social communication on the Internet augments people's total social resources by providing an added avenue for everyday social interaction. This may be true for adults, but for children and adolescents who have a very limited range of social supports at times, depending on their social involvement, it does not provide a healthy alternative. Since depressed children may want to reach out in cyberspace to form friendships, the issues of safety and quality of that friendship would, however, need to be questioned. Many Internet users believe that it has improved their lives in many ways. This has created a generation of children and adolescents who are unable to interact face to face or be socially appropriate.

Social communication on the Internet displaces valuable everyday social interactions with family and friends, and has negative implications for user psychological well-being. With reduced time spent in social activities, less time visiting with relatives and friends, reductions in their social circles, and fewer phone calls to friends and families, adolescents have poorer relationships with family and peers at school. Internet communications are less likely to support feelings of closeness with others than are face-to-face or telephone conversations. Children with depression need to feel connected through personal interaction. They need to feel the energy of the people around them.

The amount of time spent online has prompted many researchers to wonder whether it has an effect on the well-being of the child. The Internet today serves many purposes such as communication, entertainment, reference, and information. The quantity and quality of time on the Internet will influence whether the child is using it as a means to enhance his or her school work, or as a form of isolation from being involved in the real world.

Some children and adolescents may use the Internet to regulate affect, particularly, to feel better. The Internet offers pleasurable, mood-altering services and products to a variety of people. Research on affect regulation indicates that people are motivated to regulate their emotions. Those who are stressed seek escape, those who are bored seek exciting activities, and those who are depressed seek pleasure. These individuals are more likely to use the Internet to be entertained or seek escape from their present level of depression.

If used appropriately, the Internet can be a wonderful tool. Teachers and parents need to monitor the use of the Internet and where it is located. Taking the computer out of the bedroom will allow the parents to monitor where and what the child is doing online. Parental blocking of several sites may also protect the child from predators. Depressed children are targets for these individuals. Limiting the time online, monitoring the child's website visits, and increasing the amount of social interaction can only have positive effects on all involved.

Chapter Seventeen

Suicide: Warning Signs and Interventions

Suicide in children usually can be prevented if someone realizes that the child is in danger and ensures that professional help is arranged. By adult standards, the problems of children can seem insignificant. They are not. They can be just as damaging to a child as adult problems can be to an adult. Help can mean the difference between life and death. Children with depression are at an increased risk of suicide because of multiple factors that may be present in their troubled lives.

The following indicators may be warning signs for elementary-school children who may be at risk for suicide. Many suicidal children have difficulties in school and in their relationships with other children. Some feel rejected by their parents and their teachers, while others feel children are hostile toward them. Depression, particularly when accompanied by withdrawal and isolation, is a possible signal. Many have temper tantrums and become rebellious. Some run away from home. Children who are accident-prone may be at risk. Suicidal threats or a preoccupation with talk about being dead are common in children who end their lives.

Suicide is a leading cause of death in teenagers, with car accidents being second. There is some speculation that many car accidents are really disguised suicides. Some teenagers are prone to accidents. The suicidal teenager may take unnecessary risks, indulge in self-abusive behavior, or become self-recriminating and neglectful. Almost everyone who seriously intends to commit suicide leaves clues to the imminent action. The warning signs are more typical of adolescents. Suicidal threats or other statements indicating a desire to die are key indicators. It is commonly believed that people who talk about suicide do not do it. This is not true.

Before committing suicide, people often make direct statements about their intention to end their lives, or less direct statements about how they may as well be dead or that their friends and family would be better off without them. Threats of this nature, whether direct or indirect, should always be taken seriously.

The second indicator is a previous suicide attempt. Four out of five persons who commit suicide have made a least one previous attempt. Often the attempt(s) did not seem very serious. Preoccupation with final arrangements is another indicator. This may take the form of preparing a will or giving away treasured possessions.

Severe or prolonged depression may be expressed in sleep disturbances, changes in eating habits, nervousness, anxiety, difficulty in concentrating, tendency to be uncommunicative, lethargy, crying, lack of emotional response, gloom, decline in school grades or dropping out, loss of interest in friends and activities, a pervasive sense of hopelessness, and shunning friends. Depression often dulls the ability to act. As the depression lifts, the ability to act returns and earlier suicide plans can be carried out.

Changes in personality or behavior are telling as well. When accompanied by a loss or other major change in the person's life, personality and behavior change is a strong signal. The teenager may appear to have taken on a whole new personality. It is extremely important to remember that there is no suicide type. The shy person may become a thrill seeker. The outgoing person may become withdrawn, unfriendly, and disinterested.

Family structure and dysfunction play a role in a teenager's life. Disorganized home life or breakdown in the family structure will increase the likeliness that a teenager may become suicidal. Because of parental loss from death, divorce, or parental rejection, the suicidal teenager may feel loneliness and isolation or a feeling they are unloved or even responsible for the death or divorce. Studies of teenagers who committed suicide revealed a pattern of parents overtly striving for themselves and their children to be successful. While this is hardly abnormal in itself, these parents tend to compensate for their own feelings of failure, inadequacy, and insecurity. They see their children as an extension of their own fantasized successes and are likely to block out other kinds of communication from their children, especially those implying failure. These children learn early that only by being a perfect projection of their parents' fantasies will they win approval.

The suicidal adolescent may come from an emotionally deprived family in which there is a breakdown in communication. Teenagers often imitate the coping mechanisms employed by their parents: drugs, alcohol, frequent arguments, fights, threatening to leave, and threats of self-destruction. If these are the methods of dealing with stress that the parents employ, teenagers will fall into some variation of the same pattern. Facing a world of increased tension, competitiveness, pressure, and demands from parents, teachers, and peers is for some teenagers, too much to cope with and self-destructive behavior is a direct result.

Gay, lesbian, and transgender youths face the same risk factors for suicidal behavior as other youths. These include family problems, breaking up with a love, social isolation, school failure, and identity conflicts. However, these factors assume greater importance when the youth is gay, lesbian, or transgender. Suicide attempts by gay and lesbian youths are even more likely to involve conflicts around their sexual orientation because of the overwhelming pressures they face in coming out at an early age. Gay and lesbian youths may account for one-third of all youth suicides. They are two or three times more likely to attempt suicide than their heterosexual peers. Suicide is the leading cause of death among gay and lesbian youths. Initial suicide attempts related to homosexuality more frequently involved acceptance of self and conflicts with others for gay males, while lesbians tended to cite problems with lovers as reasons for attempting or committing suicide.

Self-acceptance may be especially critical for young gay males who tend to have homosexual experiences and are aware of their orientation at a somewhat earlier age than young lesbians. When these youths have gender nonconformity it elicits a negative response from others, but society seems to have a particular disdain for effeminate young males. Young lesbians face strong social pressures to fulfill the woman's traditional role of marrying and having children and may experience more depression related to failing to meet social expectations. The earlier a youth is aware of an orientation, the greater the problems he or she faces and the more likely the risk of suicidal feelings and behaviors.

Gay adolescents may be at risk for dysfunction because of emotional and physical immaturity, unfulfilled developmental needs for identification with a peer group, lack of experience, and dependence on parents unwilling or unable to provide emotional support. Gay adolescents are more likely to abuse substances, drop out of school, be in conflict with the law, undergo psychiatric hospitalization, run away from home, be involved in prostitution, and attempt suicide. The strongest causative indicators of suicidal behaviors among gay youth were awareness of their sexual orientation, depression and suicidal feelings, and substance abuse all before age 14.

It is sobering to realize that no group of people is more strongly affected by attitudes and conduct of society than are the young. Gay, lesbian, and transgender youths are strongly affected by the negative attitudes and hostile responses of society to homosexuality. The resulting poor self-esteem, depression, and fear can be a fatal blow to a fragile identity. Two ways that society influences suicidal behavior by gay and lesbian youths are the ongoing discrimination against and oppression of homosexuals, and the portrayal of homosexuals as being self-destructive.

It is the response of our society as a whole to homosexuality, and specifically those institutions and significant others responsible for their care, that poses the greatest risk to gay and lesbian youths. The vast majority of the United States still discriminates against gays and lesbians in housing, employment, and other areas. Gay and lesbian youths see this and take it to heart.

A predisposing factor in suicidal feelings among many adolescents is poor self-esteem. This is especially true for gay adolescents who have internalized a harshly negative image of being bad and wrong. For youths, a poor self-image contributes substantially to a lack of confidence in being able to cope with problems. The images of homosexuals as sick and self-destructive has tremendous effect on the coping skills of gay youths, rendering them helpless and unable to improve their situation. Gay youths who have internalized a message throughout their lives of being worthless and are unable to cope from abusive and chaotic families are at even greater risk.

Youths with poor self-esteem and poor coping skills are particularly vulnerable to suicidal feelings when confronting a problem for the first time. They do not know how to resolve it or even if they can. Gay youths are highly susceptible to suicidal feelings during their coming-out process when first facing their homosexuality amid the hostile responses it evokes in others. They may attempt suicide when they first realize they may be gay, lesbian, or transgender. Some youths deny their homosexual feelings and engage in unconscious self-destructive behavior out of self-hatred. Others try to change their orientation and make a suicide attempt when they recognize their homosexuality will not go away and is part of who they are.

Many youths realize they are gay or lesbian but attempt to hide their orientation from others. They suffer from chronic loneliness and depression. They may attempt suicide because they feel trapped in their situations and believe they do not deserve to live. A suicidal gesture may be a cry for help from these youth for others to recognize and understand their situation. Those youths who are open about being gay, lesbian, or bisexual face continuous conflict with their environments.

A final suicide risk factor for gay and lesbian youths is a bleak outlook for the future. Young people have difficulty seeing a future life that is different from the present. Gay and lesbian youths fear their lives will always be as unhappy and hard as they presently are. They do not know that they will receive any more caring, acceptance, and support than they presently receive. The little information they have about homosexuality usually reinforces these mistaken beliefs. Gay youths do not understand what life could be like as a gay male or lesbian adult. They do not have accurate information about homosexuality, positive role models to pattern themselves after, or knowledge of gay and lesbian adult communities. Lesbian and gay youths frequently do not know that many lesbian and gay adults lead stable, happy, and productive lives.

SUGGESTIONS FOR WORKING WITH THE SUICIDAL

The following suggestions are by no means exhaustive. They are strategies that have been documented and used successfully. In any type of strategy, use common sense. The specifics of the situation are paramount in the application and success of that particular intervention.

Be observant. Know and recognize possible warning signs. Pay attention to your suspicions. Trust your judgment. Take any suicidal ideation seriously. How you choose to intervene may vary depending on the situation, but any talk of suicide should, nonetheless, be taken seriously. It is important not to discount or rationalize (platitudes, ignore, etc.), thus, missing their cry for help and possibly fostering an aggressive reaction.

If you suspect someone may be suicidal, follow up. Inquire about less noticeable signs. Ask others about what they have noticed (if possible).

Do not rationalize, or discount it in your own mind. If you are unsure of what to do, get some direction from your principal, supervisor, colleague, or someone who can help. Give yourself the freedom to be direct in dealing with the situation or intent.

Approach the suicidal person, and let them know you are concerned for him or her. Hear what he or she is saying. If the person denies anything is wrong, you may want to point out some of the things you have been noticing. It would be helpful to present yourself as stable and positive in order to help bring stabilization, and control to the person. Take the risk of being personal. Try to be stable, positive, and calm. The individual is not in control so you need to be in control. Do not lose patience or be shocked by what he or she is saying. Realize that others may back off from this child or adolescent. Do not discount, challenge, criticize, or moralize, as this may spur the adolescent to destructive activity. For some, this is the last means of trying to communicate their desperation and pain.

At some point in the conversation, ask the adolescent or child if he or she has thought of, or is thinking of, killing himself or herself. Be candid. Mentioning suicide will not give the individual the idea. In fact, your verbalization of it may be a relief to him or her. Normalize the child's or adolescent's feelings without discounting them. They are not abnormal, alone, or crazy. If the child or adolescent does admit to thinking of suicide, you should explore his or her plan and means. The more detailed these are, the more the possibility of suicide exists. Ask about previous attempts and ideations. Do not discuss whether suicide is right or wrong. If a suicide plan is in process, try to reverse it or buy time until help arrives.

Explore what led to these feelings of suicide. Normalize the child's or adolescent's feelings. Help establish clarity of the problems as concretely as possible. Ask direct questions. Get to specific problems. Explore the person's resources, assets, and strengths. How has he or she handled things in the past? Offer support and realistic hope. Identify other supports such as parents, friends, family, crises lines, etc. Help to establish clarity of the problem and explore alternatives and options. This will reduce the apparent hopelessness, alienation, and aloneness, and create adaptive change.

You may want to contract with the suicidal child or adolescent. Arrange to do something tangible and meet with him or her soon after. If there is imminent danger of suicide, do not leave the child or adolescent alone. Call the police or drive the child or adolescent to the emergency department at your local hospital. If there is no imminent danger, write up a contract not to commit suicide. Align yourself with the child's or adolescent's desire to live. Clarify that you cannot be with him or her 24 hours a day and that the child is responsible for the choices he or she makes. What you can let the child know is that with or without the threat of suicide, you will be there for him or her and the child does not need to use any threats of suicide as a way of getting attention; it is understood you are available to him or her.

Do not get sworn to secrecy. If you do, break it. If a child or adolescent tells you that he or she is considering suicide, consult with a supervisor, principal, partner, other adults, and even call 911. Do not, under any circumstances, deal with this on your own. Suicidal children and adolescents have high potential for turning others away from themselves merely by what they are planning or talking about doing. They have intense feelings of anger, depression, and hopelessness. They may display various acting-out behaviors as a way of pushing you away. These children have limited abilities to communicate, the threat and/or attempt of suicide being their last and possibly only mode of communication. You need to stay present and open to communication; help the child or adolescent know that you are seriously invested in helping him or her resolve the situation and that you will not abandon the child in his or her time of crisis. Sometimes this belief of getting help is enough to save the child, or to prevent him or her from acting out in a self-destructive way.

We can substantially reduce the risk of suicide among gay and lesbian youths. The problem is clearly one of providing information, acceptance, and support to cope with the pressures and conflicts they face growing up homosexual. However, in addressing their concerns, we confront two issues of greater magnitude: the discrimination against and maltreatment of homosexuals by our society, and the inability of our society to recognize or accept the existence of homosexuality in the young. The homophobia experienced by gay youths in all parts of their lives is the primary reason for their suicidal feelings and behaviors. It is no longer difficult to document the violence, shame, and hatred by society with which lesbian and gay youths have lived. This is the issue we must address to save the lives of gays and lesbians.

We each need to take personal responsibility for revising homophobic attitudes and conduct. Families should be educated about the development and positive nature of homosexuality. They must be able to accept their child as gay or lesbian. Schools need to include information about homosexuality in their curriculum and protect gay youths from abuse by peers to ensure they receive an equal education. Social services need to be developed that are sensitive to and reflective of the needs of gay and lesbian youth.

Suicide is an ending. The ending of a young life! Society stills sees this act as one of shame and desperation. It highlights the fact that people are weak and could not make it. It denigrates individuals who do not have the proper coping skills to stick it out. Parents and teachers must examine their practices of dealing with their children or students. Are you, the adult, creating so much helplessness and hopelessness that a child will want to take his or her life as the only solution to solving the situation that you are inflicting upon him or her?

The solution to preventing suicide in the young is to change the adult behaviors and teach our children and adolescents no matter what the situation or crisis, there will always be an adult, an answer, or a way to deal with the problem. Nothing is worth ending a life for.

Chapter Eighteen

Thirteen Guidelines to Success

In our present day, there are a substantial number of children and adolescents who are suffering from depression and its associated disorders. Schools can assist students with depressive disorders by implementing interventions and consulting with school personnel and the larger school environment. The following is a series of guidelines to help in that process.

Guideline 1: Collaborate with parents, school staff, physicians, and mental-health practitioners. Depressive disorders are best treated with a comprehensive approach involving all of the above individuals. There must be a collaboration of services to ensure that the interventions are sufficient and effective when dealing with individual students. One of the concerns is that all the needs of the depressed student can be met within a school environment. This is often not the case because of limited services or counseling personnel available. Close collaboration with out-of-school mental-health practitioners such as psychologists, social workers, and licensed professional counselors can lead to better and coordinated services. There are several ways to develop collaboration with these out-of-school personnel, such as letters, phone calls, wraparound meetings, parental involvement, and contact.

Guideline 2: Construct a relationship. Depressed students need positive adult relationships. This is partly because of their social difficulties and lack of social connections. Children with depression are more likely to hear adults who offer positive encouragement. The development of a caring relationship can be viewed as a prerequisite to the student's acceptance of a variety of treatment techniques and models. If students develop a strong working alliance with school personnel, a rapport will develop and students may seek help in times of crisis or difficulty.

It is possible for all teachers to take some actions to strengthen their relationship with depressed students. For example, teachers can make a point to address depressed students by name, and make some type of personal comment to the student during every class period. Teachers can educate themselves about depression and/or ask for guidance from school counselors. Teachers should become familiar with the signs and symptoms of depression and, therefore, not react so quickly to the manifestation of these symptoms when shown by a student. By developing a caring relationship, they are more likely to look past the irritability and continue interacting positively with the student.

Guideline 3: Expand awareness of feelings. Students with depression may not be aware of why they feel the way they do. For example, an angry student may not be aware that sadness is fueling his or her anger. There are simple techniques that can be used to help build self-awareness: the following strategies are emotional vocabulary, emotional pie, and emotional thermometer. The emotional vocabulary technique involves using cards to identify emotions where the child identifies the emotion, what it feels like, and gives an example. The emotional pie technique involves drawing a large pie circle and partitioning out emotions for the week, such as his or her sad times, happy times, etc. The emotional thermometer is where the child indicates on a large thermometer the intensity of emotion he or she experienced in a particular situation. It is imperative that all adults model appropriate ways of disclosure of feelings and help guide students through the process of conversations and understanding their emotions.

Guideline 4: Emphasizing the connection among events, thoughts, and feelings. One of the ways students with depressive disorders can begin to change mind-set and feel as if they are more in control of their moods is by learning that there is a connection between what they think and what they feel. Additionally, they realize that changing the way they think about a situation can affect how they feel about it. These connections can be further explored by keeping a diary in which they record the situations they are in, how they felt in each situation, and what was going through their minds at the time. Each week this journal can be reviewed to teach about connections and negative thoughts leading to difficulty in coping.

Guideline 5: Challenge pessimistic and constricted thinking. There are many connections between what a person believes about himself or herself and that person's ability to solve problems. Depressed individuals tend to have a negative view of themselves, the world, and the future. They tend to view their failures as being due to personal failings, while refusing to take credit for their successes. Research suggests that depressed children base their self-esteem on selected areas of competence, thereby undervaluing other areas of strengths.

Challenging pessimistic children's beliefs can be best done by using a variety of behavioral cognitive strategies. School personnel can have the child evaluate his or her thoughts for errors in thinking, black-and-white thinking, all-or-nothing thinking, and questioning the evidence of a particular situation. Helping children develop new thought patterns will require practice and direct teaching of positive statements that they can say to themselves in situations that typically elicit depressive feelings. It would prove to be beneficial if all the adults in the child's life learn how to redirect the child's thinking patterns and guide the child toward more self-questioning when it comes to these thoughts.

Guideline 6: Create a network of support. Supportive networks have shown great promise in helping children and adolescents be more successful in managing their disorder. Social isolation, low levels of social support, and social difficulties are common correlates of depression. The establishment of positive social relationships is an important part of an intervention program for a depressed child or adolescent. Fostering supportive relationships between depressed students and teachers, coaches, police-liaison officers, school nurses, and other involved adults can provide depressed students with the sense they are not alone and have supportive and caring adults ready to reach out to them in time of need or crisis.

Another group that may provide access to a social network is a peer-support group. Some students may find it easier to speak with their peers about some of their issues. Overall, the message is involvement, and not isolation. School personnel need to be aware of how they foster that involvement and inclusion.

Guideline 7: Maximize opportunities for success. A useful intervention for depressed students is to increase the amount of positive reinforcement they receive. One way to do this is to increase the amount of success they have in school. All school personnel can be involved in creating opportunities for success. Possible strategies range from providing extra after-school tutoring to changing desk placement, test modifications, and homework adaptations. Depression has effects on memory, so providing children the opportunity to relearn and practice the material on several occasions will make it more likely that they will master it or recall it. Encouraging students to use learning strategies rather than relying on rote memorization is more likely to yield success.

Students with depression have negative academic self-concepts. It would be helpful for classroom teachers to give students the message that success in class comes from putting in the effort to learn skills, rather than from just being intelligent. Rather than fostering a competitive classroom atmosphere, teachers could strive to emphasize a mastery learning approach.

Guideline 8: Build social skills. Students with depression have poor social relationships. Improving their social competence by teaching social skills makes good sense. Social skills can be taught a number of ways. The use of role play can help the child understand new and difficult situations and help them discuss the appropriate social skills. Students can be taught how to communicate with a social vocabulary of individualized phrases that can be used to initiate conversations, maintain conversations, and deal with interpersonal conflict.

Children can learn how to build and maintain friendships in ways that will lead to a better quality of interpersonal relationships. Guiding the child through the social behaviors with which they are having trouble will enable them to understand their own behaviors and how these behaviors impact their well-being, and their social interactions.

Guideline 9: Provide concrete evidence of work performance and improving skills. Depressed students tend to view their world through the lens of negative expectations and low self-esteem. They tend to discount or distort any positive comments given to them. A way to help the child see the positive in a situation or the positive result of their effort and work is to provide factual, objective, concrete evidence of success. This can be accomplished through a variety of feedback strategies, including daily records, bar graphs, number of books read, skills mastered, etc. The providing of evidence helps the depressed child to see the accomplishments in a very real way.

Guideline 10: Increase engagement in pleasant events. Adolescents are more likely to be involved in activities which they find fun and pleasant. One intervention that works well for children this age is to list 10 events or activities they enjoy, and set a goal of engaging in at least one of those activities every day. These activities can be whatever the child or adolescent likes, rather than an adult's choice. Students also should be encouraged to reward themselves for successful completion of these activities. A daily or weekly chart may be kept to help the child have a variety of positive and fun activities.

Guideline 11: Increase level of physical activity. There is documented evidence that increased physical activity leads to improvements in depressive symptoms. This can be accomplished by developing and maintaining a regular exercise program. Having an exercise partner can help to increase compliance with the exercise plan and build social relationships. This is also a great opportunity for physical-education teachers to become involved in adding more fun ways by which to incorporate physical activity.

Guideline 12: Provide education about depression. Depression can be a mysterious, unpredictable disorder. Learning more about the typical signs, symptoms, causes, and treatments can help depressed students make sense of what they are experiencing and provide them with hope that they can overcome depression. Information on depression can be given to students, teachers, and parents via special programs or guidance lessons, or even in literature form.

Guideline 13: Be flexible about work expectations. Depression often impedes academic performance, energy level, and concentration. There may be times when students with depression are simply unable to keep up the normal workload. Providing these students with flexibility and understanding regarding work expectations can prevent them from entering a downward spiral of becoming further and further behind at school. Many depressed students qualify for Section 504 of the Rehabilitation Act of 1973, and, therefore, can receive a written plan that includes simple, concrete accommodations.

The 13 guidelines presented are a small percentage of possibilities that may be put in place for students with depression. Substantial numbers of children and adolescents have or are experiencing depressive disorders. More research is needed to further identify and validate school-based interventions for students with depressive disorders. There needs to be more of a relationship with how research and practical, usable, specific interventions that can be employed in school are discovered and implemented to the success of all.

Chapter Nineteen

A Personal View of Depression

CASE 1

Subject: Jennifer
Location: Littleton, N.H.
Age: 23
Occupation: Student

I was born and grew up in Littleton, New Hampshire. I was born there. It is a small town of 6,000 people, where my parents (who have been together for 30 years) have lived the majority of their lives. My brother is two years younger than me. I had a very stable home life, a very traditional, normal upbringing. I was a straight-A student throughout my school years. I had a lot of pressure to be the best I can be.

Depression crept into my life freshman year of high school. I was 14 years old. It started with a form of obsessive-compulsive disorder and anxiety disorder called trichotillomania, then I realized I had some major OCD symptoms like counting and checking and that type of stuff. Through all of that, I started to realize that it wasn't just the OCD. I was also depressed. I went to a social worker. We talked and realized there was a little more depth in what I was dealing with and why I was dealing with it. I realized it was not just the anxiety, but the depression and my feelings that I was internalizing.

As I started to go through high school, there were little things like sports and academics and always being the president of something. When it came to choosing colleges, that's when it started to get really bad. I was a junior and was dealing with college applications. Applying to seven colleges and getting into only two was devastating and disappointing for me.

My parents added pressure to succeed. This caused me to put pressure on myself. The crash didn't happen until I went to college. I didn't realize until probably two years ago that my father was severely depressed. There is a genetic link and this isn't something that was always talked about. My father was using alcohol as a depressant, but he also was very depressed and very internal about it. There is the biological link, but I think mine started situational.

I did not want to go to the University of New Hampshire because I did not think it was good enough for me. I was very unsure of what I wanted to do with my life. I stayed there for three years, each year getting a little bit worse, each year going to a lot fewer classes, and each year becoming more depressed. I slept all day, and didn't want to talk to anybody. I was on Paxil. The physician eventually upped me from 20 milligrams to 40 milligrams, thinking that was going to help. At that time, I did not know who I was and what I was doing. I just shut off. The three years were awful.

I went to a counselor two times, I just didn't feel she was helping so I stopped going. That was a part of me shutting down. I would sleep all day, and would stop making contact with people trying to help. I took medical leave from the university. It was supposed to be just a semester but I decided that I needed to move.

I moved to Arizona thinking the sunlight would help, and I would come back from it a new person. I found out what I wanted to do and I think that gave me a clear head. I still have OCD and trichotillomania and am sometimes depressed, but nothing like before. I am back down to 20 milligrams of Paxil.

I think the biggest challenge was dealing with family members who didn't understand. They were not accepting of the OCD and hair pulling. They were very angry. They didn't know how to deal with the hair pulling and didn't know why I was doing it because it was making me not look right. As far as the depression, they didn't understand why I felt that way. They did not want to accept it because we came from this happy childhood, this happy family. They had no idea how it could have happened. They also started to blame themselves a little bit, which made me feel worse. I didn't want anyone to blame themselves for something that could be genetic.

Another struggle was daily activities. I went to class but I was not happy in the classes I was taking because I did not know what I wanted to do. I felt like it was a waste of time. I gave up, and just stopped going and go to exams and be done with it, which was also harder for the family since I had been an overachiever.

I had a couple of boyfriends, but they just did not want to or could not deal with how depressed I was. I lost the relationships, and they blamed me for being miserable. I had one friend who would get me out of bed and make me go to classes. We would walk the mile to class and she would go off to her class and I would go off to mine. When she was far enough away I would turn right back around and go back to bed. It was very difficult. I connected with one person who had hair pulling and depression. We connected very well, but I felt that other people could not understand, which made contact very difficult. I am not great about calling and I think it drives them crazy because I just cannot. I just don't feel like calling and it is hard to keep friendships that way.

I never had suicidal thoughts, but I found out my brother started to have them last year. My father has had them. These are things I am finding out in the last two years. No one wanted to open up about it until I was so open. I did drink while on medications. I knew how awful that was, and how much it intensifies the effect. I also found out over the past two years that my father is an alcoholic. Everything came in a circle. Since then, I do not drink. I have gone out a few times but I don't drink because I know that it is in the family and I know how detrimental it can be. At the University of New Hampshire, I was in a sorority and did drink. We had a good time, but I made poor choices.

When I was in high school, depression was difficult because we didn't have school-adjustment counselors. I hear there are positions for school-adjustment counselors, and I'm thinking maybe I want to do that to help children. I think that a school-adjustment counselor would have been helpful. I had a mentor, my tennis coach, who ended up being principal. He was there for me. If that would have been the case all along, I could have talked and been okay. I went to a social worker, but it just didn't help. She tried to analyze me and it wasn't helpful. I think you need to make a connection.

I shut off. I am one of those people who likes to crack jokes at myself. Part of putting myself down makes me feel better. I do not know how that really helps, but I still do it. That is a part of my personality, and that's not really healthy. I didn't talk about it. I didn't want to talk about it. My mother is my best friend, and I can talk to her a little. She did not understand, so when I talked to her, it became frustrating. She would get angry at me, and I would get angry at her. It was hard to express the secrets I was thinking or feeling.

None of my teachers noticed that something was wrong. I stopped going to classes. I had one professor at the university I made a connection with in three years. It was a classics course, a major of mine. I told him my story, and to this day I e-mail him and he'll say, "How's the family?" He knows that was one of the main reasons why I crumbled. Other than him, not one else recognized my depression.

In high school, my principal knew the story. I was No. 2 on the tennis team, was athletic, and was president of student government. I had my hands in everything. I signed on to be part of the council to hire police officers for the town, and worked for the chamber of commerce. People saw me as a poster child for success. They did not think anything was wrong because I hid it.

Some people just don't know about depression. They do not know what to look for. I think that educating people and having them read valid sources and understand depression is okay. There is cause to be concerned with people who are suicidal. It is something to work through and try to help with, especially not to be afraid. By educating myself and studying depression, I became aware of what I needed to do. I think that if other people around me would have done the same, it would have helped. It is hard coming from a small town where people do not see a lot of gays and lesbians, and/or different cultures and races. You are thought of as being middle-class white, and nothing is wrong, and that's it.

I think teachers need to know the symptoms, the little things that may be overlooked in the classroom. It would have been hard for anyone in the high school to know I was depressed because I appeared outwardly happy. Awareness of all the different types of disabilities, anxiety disorders, and depression should be addressed because a lot of people are under pressure. Begin to know the families, and understand the students, and basically understand the different ways people can act out in depression.

Many parents do not want to hear that their child has a problem, which was my case. I asked my parents to read a chapter in a book about OCD. It helped them to understand that telling me not to do something was not going to help. If there is a counselor, psychologist, or psychiatrist available, maybe the child should meet with them alone to talk of things about which they are not comfortable. There should be a meeting with the parents so they can understand what their child is going through. Communication between parents and teachers needs to be ongoing as well. If a teacher starts to see a child having difficulty, he or she should speak to the parent if the child's behavior is off, or if there is a pattern of behavior developing. Being aware of a child's depression may lead to earlier interventions.

Parental denial is an issue. I tried to get my parents to understand depression, but it was like shoving it down their throat. They did not want to believe it, only that I was a good kid. How could depression happen in my life? They did not want to admit or want to tell me about my father's depression. It wasn't something to be discussed. Time was the only factor that made them understand what I was going through. After I got on medication, they were a little more accepting, and realized depression is a chemical imbalance and not just social. They were a little bit better with that; it was scientific proof and not something that they did wrong in raising me.

More people are depressed today than we know. I don't have any idea why this is happening. People know the suicidal aspect. You know you hear people say how selfish suicide and cutting is and say, "How could you do that?" No one knows until they are actually in that situation. Society is more accepting now because there are so many people who are experiencing depression.

If I had the chance to talk to teens about my experience, I would tell them that it is okay to be depressed. I would also give them strategies, or telephone numbers of agencies, and reading material to let them learn about depression. I would also reaffirm that they are not abnormal, or even so different from their peers, but that they are dealing with things differently and can survive. You can get through it. I did not think I could. I know people who cannot get through it and will always be on medication and in need of a counselor. Just let them know that they are still accepted and are not outcast because of the depression.

When I was let loose in college, that is when depression hit. I did not have someone watching over me. If there was a program after school, children with difficulties could get together, or meet at an office designated for issues. If students have a problem, they should leave class, go to that adult, and get it out rather than falling asleep in class or skipping school the next day.

Medications are always a controversial choice for many. According to my parents, I did not need medication. Paxil has been great for me in some ways and not in others. I would say it is helpful to try medication to determine what is best for the child. I think mine helped with anxiety issues, but it also zoned me out. I was nonchalant. Situations did not affect me like they used to. I was still depressed, so they increased the medication to 40 milligrams. I did not get too upset, but I also did not get really happy, and that was the problem. It is hard to balance out. I was a lot more mellow, but it was preventing me from feeling full emotion. That's why today I am trying to get off it and see if I can live my life. Behavior therapy may help me.

Treatment for me may take alternative routes. I have depression, but also have hair pulling and OCD. I know that with hair pulling and OCD, behavior therapy and medication have been very good for me. The depression is helped less so. No one has really given me good suggestions with behavior therapy for depression. I would be willing to try and see what could happen. It is hard for me as a woman because if you want children, you cannot be on medication before and during birth. Women go off medication before pregnancy and then have breakdowns, which affects the children they are carrying. That is one problem with medication that worries me. I do not want to take a pill every day of my life.

My advice is to get early intervention, to understand you are okay, that there are people around you going through the same thing, and that with understanding and education you and your family can get through it. It is difficult for some people if they do not have a supportive family to guide them through the devastation. My family is now very supportive. Just knowing you are not alone and understanding that there are ways of getting out of depression is a safety net for survival.

CASE 2

Subject: Mary
Location: Small town, New Hampshire
Occupation: Parent

My experience has been a combination of depression with bipolar disorder. My son is 11, but when he was three years old we started seeing signs of agitated behavior. At the time, we were told by many that it was normal three-year-old behavior. We questioned it, but the behavior continued. Finally, at five years old, we had him evaluated by a psychologist, who told us nothing was wrong. I did not buy this report for a second. I knew something was going on, but we did not know what.

The diagnosis for bipolar disorder didn't happen overnight. In the beginning, we saw aggressive and oppositional behavior. At mealtime, a simple request of, "Please turn the television off and come and eat," provoked an elevated response. He would argue with us but take it to a level most normal children would not. It would turn into an all-out tantrum. This went on for a long time and he would experience cycles. Sometimes the behavior was very compliant and all of sudden not, for no apparent reason.

When he was about six or seven years old, it started escalating into regular tantrums. He would be thrashing, kicking, screaming, biting and saying, "I hate you, I want to kill you." It would always end after the struggle in tears and then he would always be extremely remorseful. The depression really did not really show itself until he was about six or seven years old.

He started doing some odd things, where he would be driving in the car and he would open up the door and say, "I am going to jump out." One does not know how to react. You do not know whether you should say, "Don't you dare," or you ignore it. We ended up putting the child lock on so he could not open the door, until he got older and that did not work any longer. We took him to a psychologist in Manchester who said, "Well, clearly, he has some behavioral issues. Let us work on behavioral modifications." When you have somebody with depression, is bipolar, and has all the clinical signs of depression, modifying the behavior with just a few positive reinforcement strategies is not going to work.

After six months, the modifications were not working. At one point I said, "It doesn't matter what reward you give him, because he was always remorseful after and he is always willing to accept his punishment." When he had sessions he would try to throw himself down the stairs or open his bedroom window and threaten to jump out.

There were days I couldn't even get him out of his pajamas to go to school. It wasn't because he didn't like school because once he was there he was okay. We just had a lot of opposition when it was time to get up and get ready for school. The teachers did not see the behaviors like we saw them at home. I would go to them and say, "Are you noticing anything about Kevin? How are his behaviors in school?" They would have a shocked look and say, "Wow, such a great little boy." We would say, "What are we doing wrong? Is it us?" Nobody believed that anything was wrong with him for the longest time. A lot of our friends would say, "He is the sweetest boy in the world."

I remember questioning his math abilities in first grade and saying that he was struggling at home. They would say, "He is doing fine. It is first grade. Relax. Do not expect too much out of him." He would come home and his math took him an hour (when it should only take 10 minutes) and we got tears and tantrums over homework. He held it together at school, but when he came home, he let loose. At the end of first grade, I really had some concerns over his ability. I did not know if he was ready for second grade. He was also young, as his birthday is early September. He was the youngest one in his class. Teachers did not agree with me for the first two years. I had him tutored over the summer, and then in third grade all hell broke loose. In the meantime, we had started seeing a psychiatrist. They put him on Prozac. For the first year, it was experimental in terms of medicating him and assessing. When he entered in the third grade, he crashed and went into a downward spiral.

We saw the depression the most when he was in third grade. He would come home and start crying. When I asked, "what was the matter," it would be something trivial, such as "I dropped my book" or something like that. It would just set himself off into tears. He started realizing he was different. He was a boy, but wanted to be a girl. He started noticing his peers were not nice to him. That's when we saw the depression the most, especially the tears. He was not really socializing with peers. Again, through it all, I cannot say the teachers noticed the depression or made recommendations. I knew and said "we needed to have him evaluated." At that point, we were in such turmoil that I was willing to try anything.

I knew that Dartmouth Hitchcock had a fantastic reputation and I was putting my trust there. I would not have put my trust on anyone. I did my homework. There were certain facilities around our area that I researched. Since we were at Dartmouth Hospital, there was a trust level there that I had that I might not have somewhere else. We had been seeing the same physician for a couple of years. In the beginning, they said to give Prozac a try because the other drugs for bipolar were very invasive in terms of their side effects, and Prozac had much less of a side effect than others. That's why we decided to go with the Prozac in the beginning. Then we had Kevin evaluated at Johns Hopkins for gender-identity disorder. They also said he was severely depressed and they felt he needed to be treated further. We went back to Dartmouth and discussed it. They started putting him on the antidepressant Effexor. It helped with the depression, but it took us another six to seven months to stabilize his moods. He was all over the place emotionally. Kevin crashed and was on the verge of hospitalization again. We experienced extremely aggressive behavior and defiance.

In third grade when he was crashing, the teachers finally started noticing. I do not know if there was a specific trigger, but a likely part of it was his self-realization that he was different. Another part of it was his friends. The dynamics of his friendships were changing. Some his friends since kindergarten no longer wanted to be his friend, and that was tough for Kevin. The schoolwork was more challenging and he struggled with that. A lot of different things came together at one time and it was too much for him. Chemically, there were changes going on, too.

We kept him back in third grade. We had him evaluated, and it was revealed he had learning disabilities in math and in other areas. The independent psychologist felt that the school should provide an individual education plan in math. The school has worked hard to help him, but I feel they do not have a good understanding of bipolar disorder. There are certain factors that trigger him. If he is tired, he is really susceptible to having problems. If somebody confronts him with, "You, you need to do this now," that will not have good results. He goes up this ladder of agitation, followed by an outburst. I have told Kevin's teachers about if they see him start playing with things, that is a sign that something is going on, and if they confront him and try to push him more, he goes up the ladder as opposed to redirecting.

He really depends on structure and routine, as most children with these disorders do. When he gets to middle school and is changing classes all the time and encountering different kids (not necessarily his friends), I think he is going to become very anxious. He has been anxious about this transition since the beginning of the school year, and is talking about how nervous he is to go to middle school. I'm expecting some anxiety with that. He has been nurtured quite a bit where he is, though not necessarily academically. I think they could do more for him, but the teachers are very nurturing in the sense that they encourage him, and if anyone is bothering him, they interfere. They look out for him and make sure no one is picking on him. He likely will not get that when he goes to middle school.

Probably the biggest fear I have is not necessarily related to the bipolar disorder and depression, but more related to the gender-identity disorder. He has been with these children since kindergarten, and they pretty much accept him now. All of his friends are girls. Kevin does not hang out with the boys, yet the boys do not bother him because they have known from the beginning that he is different. When he goes to the middle school, where five different schools come together, I don't think that is necessarily going to be a positive thing.

Kevin has been stable for almost two years now. We have had two tantrums in two years, which I think is a success. We have been on an even keel, relatively speaking, but it's never perfect. You cannot get angry and frustrated and punish them because it just going to elevate it. I'm not perfect and I know how to push buttons. Inevitably, you always do what you do not want to do and react in some way you do not want to. The issue of one parent tolerating more than another and getting frustrated with each other is what we deal with. Physically, it is tough. When he was four, five, six and seven years old, he was thin and small and I had no problem putting his hands behind his back and legs over him and saying, "I'll sit here until you are done." At his worst two years ago, he had a lot of weight gain because of his medication and there were times his moods were elevated to the point I had to restrain him. I had a tough time because I am small.

There was one time when he was trashing things in the house that I told him if he kept doing that I would have to restrain him. One of the things his therapist suggested I do if I had to restrain him was to put a towel around him so he could not get his arms out. I tried doing that and, of course, we were going all over the floor. He weighed 80 pounds and in the process of us rolling around, he got a bloody nose. I tried to calm him down. Of course, when your blood pressure is up, you bleed more, so he was bleeding everywhere. I was worried he was going to pass out so I said, "You need to calm down." He replied, "No, I am not going to calm down." Finally, I called 911 because I did not know what to do. He told them I punched him in the nose, so not only did I have emergency personnel at my house, but also police. That was a scary situation.

It has been challenging in terms of siblings. Kevin has a younger sibling, and the younger sibling just did not know what to do. If my older son was doing great, everyone was doing great. If my older son was not doing great, everyone else went through hell. A lot of times he took it out on the younger one. When his moods were okay, there was no problem. When he started to getting agitated, we would immediately separate them. For a while they shared a room. At 10 p.m. when the older one is throwing a full-blown tantrum and the other one wants to sleep, that is challenging. My husband had to restrain my older son and I had to sit with my other child. It scared my other one. He didn't know what was going on. It also affected him in the sense that even though my older son was getting negative attention, he was still getting attention and the younger one felt left out. It was tough to balance the attention, how much each was getting and how to do that. I still see some issues with my younger son because of it. He is always looking for approval. Maybe that would be a part of his personality anyways, but he seems to always feel left out. He is not, but he does feel that way. With the onset of adolescence, I am going to cross my fingers. I am fortunate that we have a good psychiatrist. We know to keep an eye on Kevin. We know that as soon as things change, we need to start making adjustments.

If teachers were better educated in terms of what the signs are, they could be making some modifications early on, even if depression is not diagnosed and just suspected. I do not think that teachers or others realized how traumatic and debilitating depression or bipolar disorder is. Just getting out of bed for them can be the only success of the day. Going to school and being asked to do an hour of homework might not be possible that day. They need to understand that sometimes just getting up, and going to school, and doing the work for that day, is all the child is capable of handling.

Our teachers were very understanding. They knew that I am very active in the school, in volunteering on a regular basis. Other parents who are isolated might not know to take that step by talking to the teacher and saying, "He or she might not be doing a lot of his homework for the next couple of weeks because he is really struggling." In the elementary school, teachers tend to be a little more understanding than they are when students reach middle school and high school. My experience with dealing with students in high school as a teacher is of hearing many teachers say, "It's just an act. I'm not putting up with that." There is a lot less tolerance for depression. It is sad because there are so many children and youth who struggle and need help and do not get it. It's hard to know how to help them.

If I could develop training programs, I would include different teaching styles that teachers could use, because children who have bipolar disorder and depression or other illness tend to learn differently. I would give them flexibility to learn. They still need to learn the material, but there are other ways they could learn and be more successful. They should learn to be understanding in terms of homework, make modifications when needed, and learn behavior interventions. There were times when I went to school and it was all I could do to keep it together and not burst out into tears. I was lucky I had some teachers who said, "You look like you are really having a rough time. Just go home and take a deep breath. We will be okay here." That was helpful and teachers need to know how to do that.

Parents, too, need to realize that if they suspect that there is a problem, it's just not going to go away. Be proactive about it, try to do something, do the research, and do the homework. I know some parents whose kids have behavioral problems. They go to a general practitioner. I am not suggesting that that's the wrong thing to do. However, in my experience it is not always in the best interest of the child. I have always pursued a child specialist. Keep calling. Call 20 places if you have to until you can get in. Call every day. This is your child, so do everything you can to make him or her successful. This has always been my approach.

There was a period of time when we did consider whether or not Kevin would be placed or kept at home. We came very close to placing him, but we were able to regulate him on medication. The saving grace for us was that the medication worked and he was able to be on a more even keel. For me, what would make or break that decision was whether or not his safety was a question. If he were hurting himself, I would have to take the step and do that for him. If he were trying to hurt us or anyone else in our family, I would also have to act. If he were not trying to hurt us or anyone else, I could not place him.

There is not nearly enough support for parents. Depression is an isolated illness. We've lost friends because of it. When Kevin's behavior would really become apparent, close friends told me there was nothing wrong with him, and that it was our parenting. It was the way we handled it. That's pretty tough to take. It's tough especially in a small town. People look at you differently. There should be some type of support.

There are support groups out there, but they are not that close. There are support groups in Concord and Manchester. I did go to a group when my son was at his worst. They scared the hell out of me because what I ended up seeing was worst-possible-case scenarios. I did not feel my son was that bad at that point. I went to the groups hoping to hear, "It's tough, but here is what we do to cope." What I saw was parents whose children who had been institutionalized and there was not really much hope. All I could think after I left was, "Is that where we are headed?" For me, it was more devastating in the support group because I saw what the possibilities were.

My biggest fears for my son are addictions to drugs or alcohol, or that he will commit suicide. If we can make it through adolescence and into adulthood by avoiding either of these, I will consider it a success. We are fortunate so far that we have always been there and supportive and never made him feel like depression is his fault. We have talked about his illness, and he knows he has an illness. We have gone on the Internet and looked at websites. There is a fantastic book for children called *There is a Storm Inside of Me*. It explains what it is like to have an illness, and that having an illness does not make you a bad person. He will go through his tantrums and his bad moods and afterward would come down on himself worse than anyone else could, saying, "I hate myself. Why do I do these things?"

I do not let him wallow in self-pity. If parents make the child feel responsibility, or they do not let the child take any responsibility for their actions, I think both of these are dangerous. Kevin knows he has a disease, he knows he is going to have it for a long time, and he knows it is not his fault. He also knows he cannot use it as a crutch to get out of things. When he says, "I don't have to do this because it is too hard for me," my response has always been, "Everyone has problems. You have to deal with it. If you cannot do it 100%, do it to your 100%. You do not have to be perfect. You do not have to have all the answers right. You do not have to get an A. I do not care what your grade is as long as I see that you did your best."

Sometimes I look at him and just give a deep breath and walk away for 20 minutes. When I come back, he is in a better mood, and I am in a better mood. He still has to do what he originally had to do. He cannot get out of it, but at least it is a way to get him to do it without going up that anxiety ladder. My philosophy has always been that I do not care if it kills me, I am going to do everything I can to make him successful. My advice or encouragement for parents who may be in similar shoes is to do your research, read, and know more about depression. Know what you can do to help your child and don't just sit back and wait for someone to help you. Help yourself.

CASE 3

Subject: Megan
Location: Holderness, N.H.
Age: 27
Occupation: Parent and student

I grew up in Holderness, New Hampshire, and have lived there all of my life, except for two years in Plymouth. I am 27 years old. As a child, I had some depression because my parents divorced. When I grew into adolescence, I had a lot of depression. My decisions, which were based on my depression, were not very good. As an adult, I am still carrying that with me, but I am not depressed anymore.

As a child, I did poorly in school. On the outside, I was laughing and making everyone laugh, when on the inside I was really hurting. As an adolescent, my relationships with men were bad. That stemmed from my parents' divorce and has a lot to do with my dad. As an adult, I married a man that I might not have if I had not been depressed. I have been on a lot of medication, and when I had my second child and he was hospitalized, I had severe postpartum depression.

Some of my challenges were attending school while being depressed. I still had to do homework on time all through high school and college. The peers and challenges of fitting in and being liked, and then going home to two families while depressed, was very difficult. The challenges were staying in school and in my relationships. I loved my elementary teachers, but as far as being supportive, they were not. When my parents divorced, I was in the fifth grade and was calling out for attention. I asked questions that were not relevant. Instead of recognizing depression, they labeled me. I overheard the teachers talking that they had a fear I was going to drop out of school, get pregnant at age 16, and get involved in alcohol and drugs.

I had difficulty in relationships, especially with men. I was uncomfortable around certain men for some reason. It's like I could sense that the situation was uncomfortable. There was an incident in school. A man who worked there as a janitor acted very inappropriately with me. When I told some of the teachers, no one believed me because they thought either I was making it up for attention or trying to get him in trouble. They finally believed me when it went too far. I played basketball for him. He was the coach for one year, and kissed me in front of a whole audience of teachers and parents. I made a good play on the court and, as a result, I got a kiss. It disgusted me. They then recognized I was telling the truth, and he was fired.

As an adolescent, my depression manifested itself in that I would drink a lot and smoke pot with my friends. By age 17, I was an alcoholic. I was a waitress and could not go through the night without drinking. I was on antidepressants at the same time. I started taking medication at age 11. I saw a counselor outside of the school. My parents' response to my depression was minor. They were so involved in their own lives and hatred for each other that they did not focus on me.

My mother knew there definitely was a problem because I was full of hate. I would be nice to her when just she and my sister were present, but when a man came along, I pretended I was sick and the man had to go home. As I got older, I became very angry. I was angry with my father for brainwashing us, and angry with my mother because my father was filling our head with trash. I was always miserable. It could be Christmastime and I would refuse to decorate the tree. I never wanted to be home.

I hated seeing my mother with another man, but didn't want her to be with my father because of the abuse and drinking that went on. At the same time this was going on, I had an older brother I never saw. He used to protect me. My mother was very worried about me. She was scared of me and my behaviors because they were so unpredictable. I did not see my father much and when I did, we laughed a lot because I did not see much of him. When I was about 16 or 17, I was taking medicine so my depression was being regulated. I still hurt, but my parents thought I should get over it. My mother moved in with another man and it had been years at that time, so she felt there was no reason to cry over spilled milk. My father, on the other hand, still loved my mother but was so angry that all he did was join in on my pity party.

He was depressed, too, but he hid it and would not admit it. Instead he was living with his anger and inability to forgive. He has never to this day looked within himself and taken responsibility for the divorce. When I was a child, I blamed the divorce on my mother because she left my father. However, all we did was live with their abuse, them throwing things, and them fighting, and crying. It was awful and I had nightmares about this for years. My mother stayed married to a man who physically and emotionally destroyed her and their children. She finally had enough and left.

I do not think my parents got to the point where they sat back and said, "Wow, look at our daughter. She is devastated with this divorce." I was told that I just needed to accept things. My mother took me to counseling. My father, on the other hand, was angry that I was seeing someone because he had to pay half of the bill. Looking back, I think that my mother was lonely and needed someone in her life to make her happy, but I wish that the children were taken care of first.

As a child, I screamed for attention. I was a rude, loud, hateful child when I wanted to be. My mother couldn't handle my moods and was often scared. Teachers labeled me as a drop-out, and the only person I turned to was my counselor. As much as I loved it, of course, at age nine I felt guilty for going because my father always complained that he had to pay half. I turned to alcohol when I was 16. I went to a friend's house and drank until I was intoxicated, laughing, and did not care about things. This went on until I was 22.

Going to college was very difficult for me. At that time, my father and I had not talked for about a year over something silly. I was a freshman, not talking to my father, and lonely. I had good friends in college and drank with them all the time. As I said before, I have always been unlucky in decision making when it comes to men, and this is what happened when I drank. I got involved in nasty relationships and allowed myself to become co-dependent like my mother. I was comfortable dating people who had a drinking problem, and who were controlling. It sounds sick and turns my stomach now, but that was the way it was when I was younger. I thought if someone controlled me, they loved me.

In my life now, that's not the case. In fact, I have a problem with drinking. I do not like to be around people who are getting intoxicated and I do not like to smell it on their breath. It makes me feel like things are going to get out of control. My life turned around for me when I became a Christian and began attending church. The parishioners became my family and I then transferred from my school to university where I have never been so happy. For the first time, I did not have to drink to make myself or others happy. I felt good inside. I still made bad choices when it came to men, and I do not think that is ever going to go away. I knew what I wanted for myself, but the "good guys" were not for me. I attached myself to those who needed me, or needed help. What was I thinking! I went to AA, but it was not helpful for me.

As a teacher or parent, I would want to build a rapport with the student and find out what was going on behind the mask. I would want to gain trust with the student so perhaps I could be of help. I would not criticize or give detentions for the behavior. I would first want to work with the student and show him or her that I care, and care enough to want to know what will be going on when the student gets on that bus at 3 o'clock. That's the thing that bothers me the most. Some go home to abuse, and some do not have a real home, but teachers expect the work to be handed in on time and students to be on their best behavior.

I think that learning begins when the student can learn to trust and lean on someone. I wish I had had that for myself. I think some schools are beginning to have peer groups or groups that allow students to talk to each other and teachers about their lives. Schools need to take action and care enough for their students to recognize behaviors. Instead of labeling them as a drop-outs, they should take up the challenge and work with these students. Schools need to learn to recognize certain behaviors and be able to work with them. To me, the high schools did not have anything. I knew they had counselors, but that was more for seniors looking into colleges.

I wanted someone to care enough to approach me and want to listen to me. I did not want to have to go seeking and crying for someone. I felt like I would get the "just get over it" attitude. What I hated most was when my school would have big activities. I felt like it was out of control. Too many people doing games and having fun. At that time in my life, I needed structure and not chaos. I felt so down and really wanted just to end everything. I tried talking to faculty but, as I said, it was the winter games, and who was going to listen? I felt as though I was a voice no one could hear. I was shouting and not one was listening. I went home that day and told my brother about it, but he did not have ears to hear either.

I just felt like I had no one to talk to. There was no one who felt the pain I felt and every avenue I went down felt blocked. I felt like I was being a nag or a crybaby when all I wanted to do was have someone take the pain away. I wanted to know that I was not the only one that felt this way. The biggest difficulty for me was feeling isolated and different. Nothing mattered to me. My sister was also depressed, and that killed me inside. I needed to take care of it for her. But how could I? I could not even care for myself. She, like me, looked outside for help.

I am sure if I had committed suicide it would have been a surprise, but people saw me as a hateful, depressed child and really didn't know what to do with me. I am sure it would have still been a shock. I think my mother's biggest fear was not suicide, but that I was going to turn out like my father, an alcoholic. My father was the town drunk and I was on that path. I stopped going to high school because I was so often hung over. How sad I feel looking back, but I was depressed, and had little hope.

I think my mother did all she could or knew how to do. She was also going through a lot as a single parent, and dealing with my father, and his being incapable of being a "father." As a mother, I go through pain when my children do, so I am sure my mother was in a lot of pain. I could not see that then because I was swimming in sorrow. I can today. Back then, people avoided me and my outbursts. I don't think they knew how to deal with me. I would yell and scream and fight with my mother. I would fight with my mother and want my father to rescue me. The divorce and living with the abuse and lack of predictability in the home were all factors. The things I saw go on should never be witnessed by children. Watching my father chase my mother around with a stove pick and slamming her around until she hit the wall should never have been witnessed by me. Late at night, I heard them argue and heard my mother plead with him. I would run down stairs and try to save her, but was told to go back to my room. It was not so much the divorce that caused my depression, but the life up until then.

Again, I do not blame my mother for any of this. She did all she could do in her circumstances. Perhaps a divorce could have happened when I was nine, but she wanted to stay with my father for the sake of the children. I think a lot of parents want to stay married because they do not want the children to have to go through divorce.

My mother felt that we needed to keep our chins up and move forward. She looks at me as a ball of problems. She is always telling me to smile and stop being so negative. This is not the approach you can take with small children who are in pain, but as an adult I can understand it. I have my own family and children myself and need to work hard so my children are happy and not depressed. I have a huge fear of this. I want my children to be happy children and not depressed because I know what can come out of it.

Medication has been part of my life for a long time. I was put on Prozac but I do not think it worked well for me. I went on Zoloft. I then went back to Prozac and I was seeing a counselor. Now I am on Lexepro. I am doing well with it. I will always be depressed. I also take Klonopin when needed for anxiety. I also think I suffer from seasonal affective disorder. However, I do not take chances now. With the children, I would rather be on medication. In the summer I have more energy and feel better. In the winter and when it's cold, I am inside and have no energy. When it is dark, I feel depressed.

I have the fear that my marriage will not work or that it will become destructive and hurt the children. I fear that when they get older, my children will want to go other places because they do not feel comfortable at home. However, I communicate and do not let things go unnoticed. I try everything in my power to help my children. I pray that my marriage is successful and that I can instill happiness and peace in my children.

Since I was a girl, I always have had a fear of relationships and always told myself I would never get married. Now that I am married, I try everyday to make it a happy, successful one for all of us. I think I try and make them smile more and am always praising them. I do not want them to be sad. Sometimes I overdo it, but I feel that I am doing the best I can. I will take it day by day. I will start seeing a counselor on campus. By having a relationship and talking, I can get it out of my mind and find ways to deal with things.

My advice for children is that I hope they seek out people and know that there are others who go through depression. If they could express it through writing, that would help. For parents or teachers, I suggest that they recognize that perhaps the deviant behavior might be a result of something. I tell people who work with adolescents that alcohol is a cover and destructive behaviors will happen if they don't take control and choose to work on helping the students find themselves.

My advice for parents is just to be your child's biggest support. Let them cry, and listen to them. Tell them that it's okay to seek counseling. I would never leave their side. I would find a way to help them express themselves. I would share my story with them and tell them that they are not alone.

CASE 4

Subject: Angela
Location: Plymouth, N.H.
Occupation: Parent, works at a university

I grew up on Cape Cod, Massachusetts, and have been in New Hampshire for over 30 years. In all that time, I have worked in the field of education first and then in nonprofit management. I have two children. I adopted them, a biological brother and sister, who came to live with me when they were three and six years old. Their names are Chris and Tracy. Chris attends Plymouth State and is in his second year, and Tracy works in a local store.

I suspect my husband, David, was depressed all his adult life. He took his life in 1996 after problems in his job. He was not fired, but was given the option of fighting to keep his position or resign. He chose to resign. He was an alcoholic as well. He probably self-medicated. I have never been able to identify what the problem was because his family is very loving and wonderful. I would never say, "Oh that's the thing."

He grew up in poverty but he had a very rich childhood. His mother is from a family of 10. There were always a lot of loving people around. His brother and his sister are wonderful people. I have a very close relationship with his sister and neither sibling is depressed. He grew up Catholic in Massachusetts, close to the Boston diocese. I suspect that perhaps he had an encounter with a priest who perhaps molested him. I will never know. He never shared that with me. He was always carrying something very painful. Wonderful guy, but it created a lot of tension in my life because I ended up being a mediator between my husband's environment and others that surrounded us. I was always taking care of things for him. I do not know if I covered up, because I do not think it was very possible to cover up. He was a high-profile person. He was a principal of a high school, and had been in the school system for 25 years. He was very well loved. I always made excuses around his behavior, but he really was a great guy who had a serious problem. He was not well.

My father struggled with alcoholism, and used to give up drinking every Lent. He would not drink for 40 days. It was from one day to the next, stop drinking on Ash Wednesday and not start again until Easter

Sunday. It was a wonderful month and a half. I love him dearly, but he was an alcoholic.

My grandmother was depressed. She was a liberated woman emotionally and intellectually, but that was not accepted in that era. It was around the turn of the century, and she was committed to a mental institution by her husband for a period of time. In 1950, there was a decision that she should have lobotomy. My father and uncle, who were probably in their 40s at that point, met with my grandfather and said, "We don't want you to do that. We will take care of her, you don't have to live with her anymore."

She lived in a house on the property where I lived. We had a house and she had a house behind us. It was interesting because it was a real stress on my parents' relationship and on our family because she would periodically lose control completely. She had had shock therapy in the institution that probably made things worse.

I lived with mental illness for my entire life and spent a lot of time with that woman. She was wonderful to me. I never, ever, ever felt afraid or nervous around her. She would not do harm to me. She just had lapses sometimes into a space where she was talking to people I could not see. I do not think that she was that mentally ill. I talk out loud when I am frustrated. I think it was probably that more than mental illness. I think that was her way of coping. Grandmother would start screaming, my mother could not cope, father would come home from work. This was the 1950s and 1960s, so mental illness still was stigmatized. It is today, too, but it was extremely stigmatized back in that period. It was a hardship on the family. I think it created a stress on my father, who ended up as an alcoholic.

My husband David's mother was suicidal, but never succeeded. David was not, as far as I knew, suicidal, but he succeeded. It's sort of a bitter irony in the fact they came to live with us. His depression and his alcoholism were hard on them because it was not a particular normal, healthy environment for them to be in.

Our children knew David had a problem. He did not abuse them. If he abused anybody, he abused me emotionally, but he might have neglected them when he was drinking. He might not be very coherent if he was drinking, so I think they probably worried about him. He had a very close relationship with our son. It broke Chris's heart when he died. Chris forgave David right away, and David became a sort of hero to him immediately.

Now, at 17, 18, 19, he's entered into a different stage of rebellion. David died nine years ago. It took Chris six years to get past forgiving him. He just missed David and loved him so completely. David was his idol.

Chris has recently articulated all of that. He sees kids talking about their fathers and he hears from them how much their fathers taught them and he cannot relate to them. His father was not there to teach him how to shave. That was one of those big moments. Chris got a razor and did it himself. Another time was when he needed to get a jock strap and a cup for little league baseball and I was the one that went with him to do that because David wasn't there. So Chris missed that whole experience of bonding with a father, who could give him great direction.

Chris has been dealing with depression. I think it has been going on for years, but finally this year, it seems to come to the forefront. I have been dancing around the issue. I am very optimistic, upbeat, loving and supportive, and do everything I can. When I cannot correct a problem, I tend to back away from it and I think that activated Chris's problem. In September, Chris was difficult to deal with, just off the handle, and I finally called. Chris and I have a wonderful, loving relationship. However, constantly, every conversation had been erupting in anger, and I said, "There is something wrong here."

I called Chris on his voicemail and said, "You don't have to feel miserable for this. You can get medication for this about your father." He called me back immediately and said, "I think I need help." I made an appointment for him and he went. I do not remember the first drug he started to take. It had an effect on him sexually, so he did not want to stay on it. He went back to see the physician to change the medication and came to me six weeks into it and felt so good and wonderful. It was the first time that he ever felt like, "Oh, heck, it doesn't matter to me at all," instead of turning it in to every negative experience. Depression stopped over night, and he is such a changed person, and is so much happier. He switched medications, and is doing very well.

Chris's older sister, Tracy, is very independent. If she was depressed, it is complicated by compulsions. I would even go so far as to say she is obsessive compulsive. She drives a car that is loaded with junk, clothes, garbage, old tires, and yesterday's lunch. I do not think that's healthy. She did not go to college. She chose not to. She is working at a convenience store. She has come to terms with some of the issues. She has issues around her lack of boundaries and her poor choices, which are all wrapped up in that inability to press beyond a certain stage. This has cost extraordinary amounts of money, so it has affected me financially because I have helped bail her out more than once. Recently, we spent 2 1/2 hours in court. She was arrested because there is a tail light out on her car. They stopped her on the road and saw that she was driving with a suspended license because she had not paid a fine.

I have had to practice letting go of what I have no control over. As a parent, the most important thing is the support I can give my children. It is hard to let them suffer their consequences. It keeps us out of that position of fighting and screaming, and that's not healthy at all. That has been a good shift for us. We have had our relationship again. I do not think she can live with me because her problems are so vast and such an imposition on everyone around her. She has come to terms with that, but the behaviors are very difficult. She is managing to mature so the impact on my life has been financial and emotional stress, and some personal growth and development too. It's not all bad. There is a growth that has to happen in me where I cannot be personally involved. I have to step back and be a helper. That is a hard thing for a parent to accept.

Many school officials have not recognized my son's depression. He is actually identified as special needs. He has some processing problems. They are deeply rooted in self-esteem, which in his case does not exist. If he learns ABC today, tomorrow he is so unsure of himself. He would have to learn ABC all over again. That is the sort of behavior I saw when he was a child. I thought, "You have seen this before. You are not without intelligence. What is standing in the way?" It was nothing to do with memory. It had everything to do with being a foster child periodically in the first three years and witnessing abuse between the mother and partners. He was not even ready to go to school. Chris had so many emotional issues to deal with. No, teachers did not observe problems in him. I observed the problems in him, more so that his problems were on the academic side.

Chris is very easy to get along with. He has never been emotionally mature at the level of his peers, and that continues to be a problem. He had a group of younger friends last year and now he is finding that he is dealing with the issues surrounding younger people. When he was in middle school, he was beaten up so many times on the way home. He became very determined not to let that happen anymore, so he started weightlifting. He was in the sixth grade, so I have seen those kinds of problems. Chris gets victimized, but he is also triggering it. I know there is something about him that is triggering his victimization and, as a parent, I cannot comprehend that he has to get professional help.

Whether his depression is genetic or situational, I think it is a combination of both. This is a child who had observed many different traumatic life events. Let me answer the question with a statement Chris made, because I think more than genetic. Chris said he knew that he and Tracy had the same tendencies. He often wants to do something or is leaning toward making a bad choice and he stops himself. He describes it as being really frustrated with her. She's not a good role model for him. He feels she does not seem to care about him. Tracy lets her problems take over and he observes that in her and says to her, "I know I have those same tendencies, I know those are my problems, too, but I do not allow myself go there. I think consciously about those choices." It seems that by what he says and does, the depression is more environmental that biological.

A friend whose son has been very close with my son has said to me several times, "Chris did a lot of dope in high school." He smokes tobacco, regular cigarettes, and binge drinks on the weekends. I think he is out there on the weekends partying and binge drinking. He is very careful during the week not to let that affect his studies, so he has given it a compartment. One of the things I really want him to do is go to a counseling center. I have encouraged him many times to join things on campus, and have said, "Don't just go to class and party and go to class." He has not done that. He recently came to me and said he was going to do it.

I do think that one of his issues is struggling with his own sexual identity. I do not know where he is going to land on this but I know he needs to be around people who are comfortable with his quirky personality. Students are also pretty wide open when it comes to who you are. You do not have to be cool. You do not have to dress in the popular style. Chris has found that balance. Tracy, on the other hand, has a lot of issues, so she is not even ready to start scratching the surface.

There is always that fear that Chris may go toward taking his life. I worry about those things all the time: car accidents, physical actions, and drowning. He will test the limits. He jumped off cliffs at Livermore Falls. It scares the heck out of me when I think that he is taking risks. He talked to me once a while ago. He did not exactly put it in words of feeling suicidal, but I knew he was on the edge. He was a senior in high school and I knew he was really on the edge. That was the year he participated in youth weekends. Chris wouldn't miss a single weekend. This group was for young adults, he went to those every time they had one. He came back rejuvenated because that was a place where he could be real with his feelings. He has had a hard time in his senior year and in the beginning of taking his medication. I really want him to get to counseling, but he has to be the person that takes that step.

We had good academic supports in elementary school and into high school. I never imagined how hard it would be to help my kids make the transition to young adults. One of the greatest services for this community is to invest in research in helping kids understand that all that they are going through is internal. It's not their external environment, it's all happening in here. Whether it's a combination of meditation, or discussion groups, it would help students in their environment. It can give them an opportunity to interact in a more honest way. Adolescents are not supportive of each other as they grow into being adults. They are at that point in figuring out what their identity is. That means some nasty behavior is a part of it.

During this time, I was really happy to be able to call my physician's office, to have a conversation and have people interact with me, and to not have to face this issue alone. Now that they are older than 18, there are limits as to how I can help, and some of those barriers are a challenge. I am a facilitator at a church-group ministry, and two Sundays a month I spend two hours with a group of people talking about important life issues. I am in women's groups and a book group. We have diverse personal lives and talk about it.

People need networks. They cannot be in isolation. They have to have networks, and church to me is one of those networks. When my husband died, I was involved, then I stopped going, but I am not afraid to ask for therapy when I need it. We need responsible healthcare practitioners who can provide children with the best service possible without breaking confidentiality.

An interesting moment for me was when my daughter, Tracy, came home from college after several months. I said, "You need to have a job or you need to be in school. If you have a job, you need to pay rent." I don't need to take care of her the rest of her life; in fact, that would be a big disservice for her. That was a big moment for me, and a painful process for me to go through. It was so important for me to let go of trying to make things right. I cannot do that. I can only do this for myself and not feel selfish when I say, "I cannot tolerate the things you are doing, and you cannot make me."

That was an important place for the both of us to come to because now we are not struggling day to day. Removing ourselves from the intensity has allowed Tracy and I to be loving and receptive. Getting Chris on medication was the hardest thing to do. I said, "Either you do medication or you get counseling, both would be best, but you have to do one or the other." I did not know which would be right, but I did figure there was some sort of pharmacological answer to this pain. He desperately needs therapy. He desperately needs to help himself. He has taken the long route in the way he chooses to do it.

My advice is that patience is a virtue. It is so necessary to be patient and it's important to put my needs as a parent aside to hear how I can be helpful. I have my own little tape running of my expectations, and letting go of my expectations. I do not care what my son's sexuality is. I care about his well being. I do not care at this point if Tracy goes to college; she is very resourceful and she would be okay. I would love her to go because she is tremendously talented, but as soon as my expectations get in the way, our conversations are impossible. So, patience and put my expectations aside. I try to be as loving as I can possibly be and let them fail. If they need to fail to experience their consequences of their choices, so be it.

Chapter Twenty

Epilogue: Looking to the Future

The study of depression, its manifestations, and its destruction will continue to affect humanity. Even with all the advances we have discovered to make our lives easier, there is a generation of children, adolescents, and adults who are trapped in the depression. As the world becomes more technologically savvy, will we become more depressed? As relationships begin and end in alarming numbers, will more generations of depressed individuals appear? As more and more people turn to medication for help with depression, will future generations be addicted to these medications? Will generation after generation continue to develop low self-esteem and self-confidence?

The future does not look encouraging for many members of our society. There is a marked increase in depression. Unless we begin to change the way we interact with each other and within ourselves, nothing will change. The future can and will be improved if we begin by not allowing even one child or adolescent to suffer in silence. We, as educators, parents, and individuals, need to recognize the signs of depression and work to curtail it early in life. We need to foster inclusion in social relationships and bonds, to value the contributions of all, and to ensure that each individual child has a path that they can follow and be guided through by well-intentioned adults.

Depression can be fought and surmounted. It does not need to claim new victims every day of the year. It will be an ongoing fight, but a fight that may be won.

STATE MENTAL-HEALTH RESOURCES

It is important to note that these resources have been provided as information only. Under no circumstances does the author endorse any specific treatment centers or facilities. The purpose of including this section is to give the reader a place at which to begin to seek out services in the reader's home state. This list is a short summary of available services. Please consult the Internet or your local telephone book for additional service providers.

Alabama

Alabama Department of Mental Health and Mental Retardation
RSA Union Building
100 North Union St.
Montgomery, AL 36130-1410
Phone: (334) 242-3454; (800) 367-0955
Fax: (334) 242-0725
URL: www.mh.state.al.us
Type of organization: State mental-health agency.

Laurel Oaks Behavioral Health Center
700 E Cottonwood Road
Dothan, AL 36301-3644
Phone: (334) 794-7373
Type of organization: Residential treatment centers for children.

Spectracare Mental Health System Barbour/Henry County Day Treatment
403 Dothan Road
Abbeville, AL 36310-2903
Phone: (334) 585-6864
Type of organization: Residential treatment centers for children.

Spectracare Mental Health System Adolescent Residential Center
1539 Sweetie Smith Road
Ashford, AL 36312-7422
Phone: (334) 691-3978
Type of organization: Residential treatment centers for children.

Alaska

North Slope Borough Community Mental Health Center
PO Box 669
Barrow, AK 99723
Phone: (907) 852-0260
Type of organization: Outpatient clinics.

Arizona

Arizona Division of Behavioral Health Services
Department of Health Services
150 N. 18th Avenue, Second Floor
Phoenix, AZ 85016
Phone: (602) 364-8507
Fax: (602) 364-4570
URL: www.hs.state.az.us/bhs
Type of organization: State mental-health agency.

Community Behavioral Health Services
145 S. Main St.
Fredonia, AZ 86022
Phone: (928) 645-7230

Horizon Human Services Outpatient, Children & Family Services
5497 W. McCartney Road
Casa Grande, AZ 85222
Phone: (520) 723-9800
Type of organization: Multi-setting mental-health organizations.

Mental Health Association of Arizona
6411 E. Thomas Road
Scottsdale, AZ 85251
Phone: (480) 994-4407
Fax: (480) 994-4744
URL: www.mhaarizona.org
Type of organization: Services include free mental-health screenings, support groups, referrals, mentor programs, education, and advocacy.

MIKID (Mentally Ill Kids in Distress)
755 E. Willetta St. Suite 128
Phoenix, AZ 85006
Phone: (602) 253-1240
Secondary Phone: (800) 35-MIKID
Fax: (602) 523-1250
URL: www.mikid.org
Type of organization: Parent advocacy group that provides education and a resource center for parents. It also provides information on relevant support groups.

Arkansas

Arkansas Division of Mental Health Services
Department of Human Services
4313 W. Markham St.
Little Rock, AR 72205
Phone: (501) 686-9164
Fax: (501) 686-9182
URL: www.state.ar.us/dhs/dmhs/
Type of organization: State mental-health agency. Oversees nonprofit community mental-health centers.

Arkansas Federation of Families for Children's Mental Health
5800 W. 10th, Suite 101
Little Rock, AR 72204
Phone: (888) 682-7414; (501) 537-9060
Fax: (501) 537-9062
Type of organization: Parent-advocacy group.

Counseling Associates, Inc. McCormack Place Apartments
855 S. Salem Road
Conway, AR 72034
Phone: (479) 968-1298
Type of organization: Residential treatment centers for children.

Health Resources of Arkansas, Inc. Youth Center
1355 E. Main St.
Batesville, AR 72501

Phone: (870) 793-8910
Type of organization: Multi-setting mental-health organizations.

Ozark Guidance Center, Inc.
208 Highway 62 W.
Berryville, AR 72616
Phone: (870) 423-2758
Type of organization: Residential treatment centers for children.

California

Alameda Community Support Center & Children's Outpatient Services
2226 Santa Clara Ave.
Alameda, CA 94501
Phone: (510) 522-4668
Type of organization: Outpatient clinics.

Because I Love You Parent Support Group
P.O. Box 2062
Winnetka, CA 91396
Phone: (310) 659-5289; (818) 882-4881
Fax: (805) 493-2714
URL: www.becauseiloveyou.org
Type of organization: Free support group for parents of children with any type of behavioral or emotional problem. Offered in 21 states.

California Council of Community Mental Health Agencies
1127 11th Street, Suite 925
Sacramento, CA 95814
Phone: (916) 557-1166
Fax: (916) 447-2350
E-mail: mher@cccmha.org
URL: www.cccmha.org
Type of organization: State legislative body for mental-health agencies.

California Department of Mental Health
1600 9th St., Room 150
Sacramento, CA 95814
Phone: (800) 896-4042; (916) 654-3565

Fax: (916) 654-3198
URL: www.dmh.cahwnet.gov
Type of organization: State mental-health agency.

Crestwood Behavioral Health, Inc. Crestwood Geriatric
295 Pine Breeze Dr.
Angwin, CA 94508
Phone: (209) 965-2461
Type of organization: Residential treatment centers for children.

Colorado

Colorado Child and Adolescent Psychiatric Society
6000 E. Evans Ave., Bldg. 1, Suite 140
Denver, CO 80222
Phone: (303) 692-8783
Fax: (303) 692-8823
Type of organization: The organization is the contact point in Colorado for information about the activities of the American Academy of Child and Adolescent Psychiatry. It can provide referrals to child/adolescent psychiatrists in the state.

Colorado Mental Health Services
3824 W. Princeton Circle
Denver, CO 80236
Phone: (303) 866-7400
Fax: (303) 866-7428
URL: www.cdhs.state.co.us/ohr/mhs/index.html
Type of organization: State mental-health agency.

Colorado West Mental Health, Inc.
Aspen Counseling Center
405 Castle Creek Road, Suite 9
Aspen, CO 81611
Phone: (970) 920-5555
Type of organization: Residential treatment centers for children.

Pikes Peak Mental Health Center
Child & Family Center
179 Parkside Dr.
Colorado Springs, CO 80910
Phone: (719) 572-6300
Type of organization: Multi-setting mental-health organizations.

Connecticut

Child Guidance Center of Greater
Bridgeport, Inc.
1081 Iranistan Ave.
Bridgeport, CT 06604
Phone: (203) 367-5361
Type of organization: Outpatient clinics.

Community Education, Connecticut Department of Mental Health
410 Capitol Avenue, 4th Floor
P.O. Box 341431
Hartford, CT 06134
Phone: (800) 446-7348; (860) 418-6948
TDD: (888) 621-3551
Fax: (860) 418-6786
URL: www.dmhas.state.ct.us
Type of organization: This organization provides information about mental health and other support services at the state level and is active in addressing and advocating for mental-health system issues. Provides information about consumer activities.

Families United for Children's Mental Health
P.O. Box 151
New London, CT 06320
Phone: (860) 439-0710
Fax: (860) 715-7098
URL: www.ctfamiliesunited.homestead.com
Type of organization: The CT chapter of the Federation of Families for Children's Mental Health. It is a support and advocacy group for families

of children with mental-health needs. It provides information, referrals, and training for family advocates.

Family & Children's Aid, Inc.
75 West St.
Danbury, CT 06810
Phone: (203) 748-5689
Type of organization: Residential treatment centers for children.

The Village for Family & Children, Inc.
1680 Albany Ave.
Hartford, CT 06105
Phone: (860) 236-4511
Type of organization: Residential treatment centers for children.

Delaware

Brenford Place Residential Treatment Center
136 Waterview Lane
Dover, DE 19904
Phone: (302) 653-6589
Type of organization: Residential treatment centers for children.

Children & Families First
903 S. Governors Ave., Suite 1
Dover, DE 19904
Phone: (302) 674-8384
Type of organization: Residential treatment centers for children.

Children & Families First
Claymont Community Center
3301 Green St.
Claymont, DE 19703
Phone: (302) 792-2757
Type of organization: Residential treatment centers for children.

Delaware Guidance Services for Children & Youth
1213 Delaware Ave.
Wilmington, DE 19806
Phone: (302) 652-3948
Type of organization: Outpatient clinics.

Middletown Residential Treatment Center
495 E. Main St.
Middletown, DE 19709
Phone: (302) 378-5238
Type of organization: Residential treatment centers for children.

New Castle
Terry Children's Psychiatric Center
10 Central Ave.
New Castle, DE 19720
Phone: (302) 577-4270
Type of organization: Residential treatment centers for children.

District of Columbia

The National Mental Health Association maintains a referral and information center and can help you locate local chapters. These local groups have information about community services and engage in national and state level advocacy. For more information about the association, contact:

National Mental Health Association Information Center
1021 Prince Street
Alexandria, VA 22314-2971
Phone: (703) 684-7722; 800-969-6642
Fax: (703) 684-5968
E-mail: infoctr@nmha.org
URL: www.nmha.org

Florida

DMDA—Greater Jacksonville
6271-24 St. Augustine Road 3126
Jacksonville, FL 32217
Phone: (904) 730-8291; (904) 737-6788
Fax: (904) 448-8965
Type of organization: Educate patients, families, professionals, and the public concerning the nature of depressive and manic-depressive illness as treatable medical diseases; to foster self-help for patients and families; to eliminate discrimination and stigma; to improve access to care; and to advocate for research toward the elimination of these illnesses.

DMDA Fellowship for Depression and Manic-Depression
919 S.E. 14 St.
Ocala, FL 34471
Phone: (352) 732-0879
Type of organization: Seeks to educate patients, families, professionals and the public concerning the nature of depressive and manic-depressive illnesses as treatable medical diseases; seeks to foster self-help for patients and families; seeks to eliminate discrimination and stigma; seeks to improve access to care; seeks to advocate for research toward the elimination of these illnesses. Meetings are from September to May on the first and third Wednesday of each month.

Florida Department of Children and Families
1317 Winewood Blvd., Bldg. 1, Room 202
Tallahassee, FL 32399
Phone: (850) 487-1111
Fax: (850) 922-2993
URL: www.state.fl.us/cf_web/
Type of organization: The state department for alcohol, drug abuse, and mental-health services. It provides information and referrals to the public. The department oversees state legislative affairs such as rules, statutes, and revisions.

Harbor Behavioral Health Care Institute
Doris Cook Smith Counseling Center
14527 7th St.
Dade City, FL 33523
Phone: (352) 521-1474
Type of organization: Residential treatment centers for children.

Manatee Children's Services
The Flamiglio Center
439 Cortez Road W.
Bradenton, FL 34207
Phone: (941) 345-1200
Type of organization: Residential treatment centers for children.

Manatee Palms Youth Services
4480 51st St. W.
Bradenton, FL 34210

Phone: (941) 792-2222
Type of organization: Private psychiatric hospitals.

Georgia

Carter Center Mental Health Programs
1 Copenhill 453 Freedom Pkwy.
Atlanta, GA 30307
Phone: (404) 420-5165
Fax: (404) 420-5158
URL: www.cartercenter.org
Type of organization: The Carter Center Mental Health Program addresses public-policy issues surrounding mental health and mental illnesses through the Carter Center Mental Health Task Force and the annual Rosalynn Carter Symposium on Mental Health Policy. The task force identifies major mental-health issues and develops initiatives to reduce stigma and discrimination against people with mental illnesses. The symposium provides a forum for national mental-health organizations and their leaders to coordinate their efforts on issues of common concern.

Child & Adolescent Outpatient
Piedmont Hall
22 Piedmont Ave. S.E.
Atlanta, GA 30303
Phone: (404) 616-2218
Type of organization: Outpatient clinics.

Coastal Harbor Treatment Center
1150 Cornell Ave.
Savannah, GA 31406
Phone: (912) 692-4285
Type of organization: Residential treatment centers for children.

Georgia Mountains Community Services
Union MRSC, Trackrock Industries
10 Hughes St. B
Blairsville, GA 30512
Phone: (706) 745-5231
Type of organization: Residential treatment centers for children.

Georgia Mountains Community Services
Habersham MRSC, Mountain Industries
451 Roper Dr.
Clarkesville, GA 30523
Phone: (706) 754-9423
Type of organization: Residential treatment centers for children.

Highland Rivers MH Center
Fannin Child & Adolescent
3828 Appalachian Hwy.
Blue Ridge, GA 30513
Phone: (706) 632-0236
Type of organization: Multi-setting mental-health organizations.

Hillside, Inc.
690 Courtenay Dr. N.E.
Atlanta, GA 30306
Phone: (404) 875-4551
Type of organization: Residential treatment centers for children.

Lighthouse Care Center of Augusta
3100 Perimeter Pkwy.
Augusta, GA 30909
Phone: (706) 651-0005
Type of organization: Residential treatment centers for children.

National Mental Health Association of Georgia
100 Edgewood Ave. N.E., Suite 502
Atlanta, GA 30303
Phone: (404) 527-7175
Fax: (404) 527-7187
URL: www.nmhag.org
Type of organization: The National Mental Health Association of Georgia serves people with mental illness and their families by promoting mental health, preventing mental illness, and ensuring access to appropriate treatment through advocacy, education and training, research, service provision, and the reduction of stigma.

Three Springs Augusta
3431 Mike Padgett Hwy.
Augusta, GA 30906
Phone: (706) 772-9053
Type of organization: Residential treatment centers for children.

Hawaii

Behavioral Health Services Administration
Department of Health
P.O. Box 3378
Honolulu, HI 96801
Phone: (808) 586-4419
Fax: (808) 586-4444
URL: www.state.hi.us/doh/about/behavior.html
Type of organizaion: The Center for Mental Health Services awards grants to statewide, family-run networks to provide support and information to families of children and adolescents with serious emotional, behavioral, or mental disorders. For more information, contact

Hawaii Families As Allies
P.O. Box 700310
Kapolei, HI 96709-0310
Phone: (808) 487-8785
Fax: (808) 487-0514
E-mail: HFAllies@aol.com

Idaho

American Falls
Region VI Family & Children's Services
Child Mental Health Services
502 Tyhee Ave.
American Falls, ID 83211
Phone: (208) 226-5186
Type of organization: Outpatient clinics.

North Idaho Behavioral Health
Coeurd' Alene
2003 Lincoln Way, ID 83814
Phone: (800) 221-5008
Weeks And Vietri
818 S. Washington
Moscow, ID 83843
Phone: (208) 882-8514
Type of organization: Outpatient counseling center for adolescents and children with depression.

Northwest Children's Home
Syringa House
1306 E. Karcher Road
Nampa, ID 83687
Phone: (208) 467-5223
Type of organization: Residential treatment centers for children who are mentally ill or delinquent.

Illinois

Black Network In Children's Emotional Health (BNICEH)
6951 N. Sheridan Road
Chicago, IL 60626
Phone: (773) 338-1090
Fax: (773) 493-1510
Type of organization: BNICEH is a global, family-centered organization. This organization is a chapter of the Federation of Families for Children's Mental Health. It is also a member of Chicago Together, the Child Welfare and Juvenile Justice Consortium, and Urban Art Retreat Coalition.

DBSA, Fox Valley
2365 Coach & Surrey Lane
Aurora, IL 60506
Phone: (630) 859-8035
URL: www.geocities.com/foxvalleydmda/
Type of organization: Educate consumers, families, professionals, and the public concerning the nature of depressive and manic-depressive illness as treatable medical diseases; to foster self-help for patients and families;

to eliminate discrimination and stigma; to improve access to care; and to advocate for research toward the elimination of these illnesses.

Lutherbrook Children's Center
of Lutheran Child & Family Services
343 W. Lake St.
Addison, IL 60101
Phone: (630) 543-6900
Type of organization: Residential treatment centers for children.

Resurrection Behavior Health
1820 S. 25th Ave.
Broadview, IL 60155
Phone: (708) 681-2324
Type of organization: Residential treatment centers for children.

Indiana

Bowen Center
P.O. Box 497
Warsaw, IN 46581
Phone: (800) 342-5653
URL: www.bowencenter.org

Indiana Federation of Families for Children's Mental Health
55 Monument Circle, Suite 455
Indianapolis, IN 46204
Phone: (800) 555-6424, ext. 228; (317) 638-3501
Fax: (317) 638-3540
URL: www.mentalhealthassociation.com/IFFCMH.htm
Type of organization: Statewide parent-advocacy organization.

Oaklawn Association
Dr. Tim McFadden
330 Lakeview Dr.
Goshen, IN 46527
Phone: (800) 282-0809
Type of organization: Inpatient and outpatient facilities for children and adolescents who are mentally ill.

Park Center, Inc.
Decatur Counseling Services
809 High St.
Decatur, IN 46733
Phone: (260) 724-9669
Type of organization: Residential treatment centers for children.

Iowa

Des Moines Child & Adolescent
Guidance Center
1206 Pleasant St.
Des Moines, IA 50309
Phone: (515) 244-2207
Type of organization: Residential treatment centers for children.

Gerard Treatment Programs
104 S. 17th St.
Fort Dodge, IA 50501
Phone: (515) 574-5492
Type of organization: Residential treatment centers for children.

Iowa Federation of Families for Children's Mental Health
303 W. Main
P.O. Box 362
Anamosa, IA 52205
Phone: (319) 462-2187; (888) 400-6302 (family only)
Fax: (319) 462-6789
URL: www.iffcmh.org
Type of organization: Parent-advocacy group.

Kansas

DMDA—Southwest Kansas
706 W. Fair
Garden City, KS 67846
Phone: (620) 276-2198; (620) 279-0901
Type of organization: Educate patients, families, and professionals, and the public concerning the nature of depressive and manic-depressive ill-

ness as treatable medical diseases; to foster self-help for patients and families; to eliminate discrimination and stigma; to improve access to care; and to advocate for research toward the elimination of these illnesses.

Johnson County Mental Health Center
6000 Lamar Ave., Suite 130
Mission, KS 66202
Phone: (913) 831-2550
Type of organization: Residential treatment centers for children.

Johnson County Mental Health Center Adolescent Center for Treatment
301 N. Monroe St.
Olathe, KS 66061
Phone: (913) 782-0283
Type of organization: Residential treatment centers for children.

Johnson County Mental Health Center Olathe Office
1125 W. Spruce
Olathe, KS 66061
Phone: (913) 782-2100
Type of organization: Residential treatment centers for children.

Mental Health Association of South Central Kansas
555 N. Woodlawn, Suite 3105
Wichita, KS 67208
Phone: (316) 685-1821
Fax: (316) 685-0768
URL: www.mhasck.org
Type of organization: Affiliated with the NMHA.

Kentucky

Communicare, Inc.
Adult & Children's Crisis Stabilization
100 Gray St.
Elizabethtown, KY 42701
Phone: (270) 360-0419
Type of organization: Multi-setting mental-health organizations.

Kid's Care Child Development Center
1308 Woodland Dr.
Elizabethtown, KY 42701
Phone: (270) 737-5676
Type of organization: Multi-setting mental-health organizations.

Nelson County Child Development Program
327 S. 3rd St.
Bardstown, KY 40004
Phone: (502) 348-0585
Type of organization: Multi-setting mental-health organizations.

Louisiana

Abbeville Mental Health Clinic
111 E. Vermilion St.
Abbeville, LA 70510
Phone: (337) 898-1290
Type of organization: Outpatient clinics.

Broadway Inc., K Bar B Youth Ranch
31294 Highway 190
Slidell, LA 70458
Phone: (985) 641-1425
Type of organization: Residential treatment centers for children.

DePaul/Tulane Behavioral Health Center
1040 Calhoun
New Orleans, LA 70118
Phone: (504) 899-8282; (504) 582-7852
Fax: (504) 897-5775
URL: depaultulane.com/custompage.asp?guidCustomContentID=0AEF914C-9FB5-11D4-81F3-00508B1249D5
Type of organization: Teaching facility offers programs for children, adolescents, and adults. DePaul/Tulane Behavioral Health Center is well known for successfully treating difficult cases and accepting referrals from other facilities and therapists across the nation. The hospital offers free assessments and referrals 24 hours a day.

Louisiana Federation of Families for Children's Mental Health
P.O. Box 4767
Shreveport, LA 71134
Phone: (800) 224-4010; (318) 227-2796
Fax: (318) 227-2793
Type of organization: Parent-advocacy group.

Maine

Children's Behavioral Health Services
11 State House Station
Augusta, ME 04333
Phone: (207) 287-4251; (800) 588-5511
TTY: (207) 287-9915

Community Health & Counseling Services
42 Cedar St.
Bangor, ME 04401
Phone: (207) 947-0366
Type of organization: Residential treatment centers for children.

Community Health & Counseling Services
Big Red Redemption Center
12 Barker St.
Bangor, ME 04401
Phone: (207) 947-0366
Type of organization: Residential treatment centers for children.

Maryland

Mental Health Association of Maryland
The Rotunda
711 W. 40th St.
Suite 460
Baltimore, MD 21211
Phone: (410) 235-1178; (800) 572-MHAM (6426)
Fax: (410) 235-1180
E-mail: info@mhamd.org

North Baltimore Center, Inc.
Children's Program
6999 Reisterstown Road, Floor 2, Suites 7 & 8
Baltimore, MD 21215
Phone: (410) 585-0598
Type of organization: Multi-setting mental-health organizations.

Regional Institute for Children & Adolescents, Baltimore
605 S. Chapel Gate Lane
Baltimore, MD 21229
Phone: (410) 368-7800
Type of organization: Residential treatment centers for children.

Massachusetts

Child & Family Service of Pioneer Valley Easthampton Counseling/ MH Clinic
30 Union St.
Easthampton, MA 01027
Phone: (413) 529-1764
Type of organization: Outpatient clinics.

DMDA—NE/Worcester
P.O. Box 2624
Worcester, MA 01653
Phone: (508) 842-0460
Fax: (508) 421-6556
Type of organization: Educate consumers, families, professionals, and the public concerning the nature of depressive and manic-depressive illness as treatable medical diseases; to foster self-help for consumers and families; to eliminate discrimination and stigma; to improve access to care; and to advocate for research toward the elimination of these illnesses.

Germaine Lawrence Diagnostic Center
Cushing Dr. Road
Arlington, MA 02476
Phone: (781) 648-6200
Type of organization: Residential treatment centers for children.

Lutheran Mental Health
58 Centre Ave.
Abington, MA 02351
Phone: (508) 626-1500
Type of organization: Residential treatment centers for children.

Massachusetts Department of Mental Health
25 Staniford St.
Boston, MA 02114
Phone: (617) 262-8000
URL: www.state.ma.us/dmh/_MainLine/MissionStatement.HTM
Type of organization: State mental-health agency.

Michigan

Community Mental Health for Central MI Midland County Children & Family Services
3611 N. Saginaw Road
Midland, MI 48640
Phone: (989) 631-2323
Type of organization: Multi-setting mental-health organizations.

DMDA MDSG—Grand Rapids
858 Reynard
Grand Rapids, MI 49507
Phone: (616) 246-0280
Type of organization: Educate patients, families, and professionals, and the public concerning the nature of depressive and manic-depressive illness as treatable medical diseases; to foster self-help for patients and families; to eliminate discrimination and stigma; to improve access to care; and to advocate for research toward the elimination of these illnesses.

Eaton County Counseling Center
551 Courthouse Dr., Suite 5
Charlotte, MI 48813
Phone: (517) 543-5100
Type of organization: Residential treatment centers for children.

Northpointe Behavioral Healthcare System
Bass Lake Home
3025 Bass Lake Road
Iron Mountain, MI 49801
Phone: (906) 774-7809
Type of organization: Residential treatment centers for children.

Minnesota

MDMDA—Minnesota
2021 E. Hennepin Ave. #412
Minneapolis, MN 55413
Phone: (612) 379-7933
Fax: (612) 331-1630
Type of organization: Educate patients, families, and professionals, and the public concerning the nature of depressive and manic-depressive illness as treatable medical diseases; to foster self-help for patients and families; to eliminate discrimination and stigma; to improve access to care; and to advocate for research toward the elimination of these illnesses. It provides support to consumers and their families.

Range Mental Health Center
624 S. 13th St.
Virginia, MN 55792
Phone: (218) 749-2881
Type of organization: Children and adolescent center that deals with depression and mental illness.

Washington Child Guidance Center
2430 Nicollett Ave.
Minneapolis, MN 55404
Phone: (612) 871-1454

Wilder Foundation
919 LaFond Ave.
St. Paul, MN 55104
Type of organization: Children's mental-health clinic.

Mississippi

Hiends Mental Health
969 Lakeland Dr.
Jackson, MS 39216
Type of organization: Children and adolescents with depression.

Mississippi Families as Allies for Children's Mental Health, Inc.
5166 Keele St.. Bldg. A
Jackson, MS 39206
Phone: (800) 833-9671; (601) 981-1618
Fax: (601) 981-1696
Type of organization: Family support and advocacy organization. Provides respite services and some limited intensive-case management support. Also has family support and education programs.

National Alliance of Mental Health
411 Briarwood Dr.
Jackson, MS 39206
Type of organization: Focuses on adolescents with depression.

Region VII
613 Marquette Road
Brandon, MS 39043
Type of organization: Children and adolescents with depression.

Missouri

Behavior Health Care
1430 Olive
St. Louis, MO 63103
Phone: (314) 206-3700

Missouri Department of Mental Health
1706 E. Elm, P.O. Box 687
Jefferson City, MO 65102
Phone: (800) 364-9687; (573) 751-4122
Fax: (573) 751-8224

URL: www.dmh.missouri.gov/
Type of organization: State mental-health agency.

Trunman Medical Center Behavioral Health
2211 Charlotte
Kansass, MO 64111
Phone: (816) 404-5700

University Behavioral Health Services
601 Business Loop 70 W.
Columbia, MO 65201
Phone: (573) 884-1550

Montana

KIDS Behavioral Health of Montana
55 Basin Creek Road
Butte, MT 59701
Phone: (406) 494-4183
Type of organization: Residential treatment centers for children.

Mental Health Services Bureau
555 Fuller Ave.
P.O. Box 202905
Helena, MT 59620

Partial School @ Deaconess Hospital
Deaconess Psychiatric Center
Billings, MT 59101
Phone: (406) 657-3900

Yellow Stone Boys and Girls Ranch
2303 Grand Ave.
Billings, MT 59102
Phone: (406) 245-2751

Nebraska

Alegent Health Psychiatric Associates
16901 N. 72nd St.
Omaha, NE 68122
Phone: (402) 717-4673

Cedars Youth Services
640 N. 48th St., Suite 100
Lincoln, NE 68504
Phone: (402) 461-3047
URL: www.lfsneb.org

Office of Mental Health, Substance Abuse and Addictions Services
P.O. Box 98925
Lincoln, NE 68509
Phone: (800) 254-4202; (402) 479-5166
Fax: (402) 479-5162
URL: www.hhs.state.ne.us/beh/mhsa.htm
Type of organization: State mental-health agency.

Nevada

Adolescent Residential Treatment Center
480 Galletti Way
Sparks, NV 89431
Phone: (775) 688-1633
Type of organization: Residential treatment centers for children.

Children's Mental Health Consortium
Division of Child/Family Conference Room
1572 E. College Pkwy., Suite 161
Carson City, NV 89706
Phone: (702) 388-8899

N. Nevada Mental Health Advisory Board
Bldg. 1
480 Galletti Way
Sparks, NV 89431

Nevada Mental Health & Developmental Services Division
Department of Human Resources
505 E. King Street, Room 602
Carson City, NV 89701
Phone: (800) 992-0900; (775) 684-5943
Fax: (775) 684-5966

URL: mhds.state.nv.us/
Type of organization: State mental-health agency.

Nevada PEP Collaborating for Children Network
4600 Kietzke Lane, C-128
Reno, NV 89502
Phone: (800) 216-5188; (775) 448-9950
Fax: (775) 448-9603
URL: www.nvpep.org

New Hampshire

Claremont Child and Family Center
West Central Behavioral Health
18 Bailey Ave.
Claremont, NH 03743
Phone: (603) 543-5449
Type of organization: Multi-setting mental-health organizations.

DMDA–Nashua
PO Box 3761
Nashua, NH 03061
Phone: (603) 886-8520; (603) 880-9225
Type of organization: Educate patients, families, and professionals, and the public concerning the nature of depressive and manic-depressive illness as treatable medical diseases; to foster self-help for patients and families; to eliminate discrimination and stigma; to improve access to care; and to advocate for research toward the elimination of these illnesses.

Genesis Behavioral Health
771 N. Main St.
Laconia, NH 03246
Phone: (603) 524-1100; (603) 528-0305
Fax: (603) 528-0760
URL: www.genesisbh.org
Type of organization: Offers case management, therapy, psychiatry, groups, independent living, and medication management for children, adults, families and seniors. Also provides emergency treatment and sliding scale fee services to low-income clients. Serves Belknap and lower Grafton counties.

NAMI New Hampshire
15 Green St.
Concord, NH 03301
Phone: (800) 242-6264; (603) 225-5359
Fax: (603) 228-8848
URL: www.naminh.org/
Type of organization: NAMI New Hampshire is a support and advocacy organization. It sponsors local support groups and offers education and information about community services for people with mental illness and their families.

New Hampshire Division of Behavioral Health
State Office Park
S. 105 Pleasant St.
Concord, NH 03301
Phone: (800) 852-33451; (603) 271-5000
Fax: (603) 271-5058
URL: www.dhhs.state.nh.us/DHHS/DHHS_SITE/default.htm
Type of organization: State mental-health agency.

Riverbend Community Mental Health, Inc.
Children's Intervention Program
3 N. State St.
Concord, NH 03301
Phone: (603) 228-0547
Type of organization: Multi-setting mental-health organizations.

New Jersey

DBSA—Mt. Holly
1337 Thornwood Dr.
Mt. Laurel, NJ 08054
Phone: (856) 234-6238
Type of organization: Educate patients, families, and professionals, and the public concerning the nature of depressive and manic-depressive illness as treatable medical diseases; to foster self-help for patients and families; to eliminate discrimination and stigma; to improve access to care; and to advocate for research toward the elimination of these illnesses.

Division of Medical Assistance & Health Services
New Jersey Department of Human Services
PO Box 712
Trenton, NJ 08625
Phone: (609) 588-2600
Fax: (609) 588-3583
Type of organization: State Medicaid agency.

Family & Children's Services
of Central NJ MH Agency
223 State Route 18, Suite 201
East Brunswick, NJ 08816
Phone: (732) 418-7077
Type of organization: Outpatient clinics.

Ocean Mental Health Services, Inc.
Ocean Academy for Children & Families
160 Route 9
Bayville, NJ 08721
Phone: (732) 349-5550
Type of organization: Residential treatment centers for children.

Woodbridge Child Diagnostic &
Treatment Center
15 Paddock St.
Avenel, NJ 07001
Phone: (732) 499-5050
Type of organization: Residential treatment centers for children.

New Mexico

Aspen Behavioral Health
3800 Osuna N.E., Suite 2
Albuquerque, NM 87109
Phone: (505) 342-2474; (888) 912-7736
Fax: (505) 342-2454
URL: www.region5rcc.org
Type of organization: Aspen is a Behavioral Healthcare Organization that provides quality mental health and substance-abuse services for children,

adults, and seniors. In addition, Aspen created and maintains a website with a comprehensive listing of behavioral health and social services in Bernalillo County for children, adults, and seniors, with funding from the New Mexico Department of Health.

DMDA—Albuquerque
P.O. Box 27619
Albuquerque, NM 87125
Phone: (505) 889-3632
URL: www.dbsa4albq.org
Type of organization: Educate patients, families, and professionals, and the public concerning the nature of depressive and manic-depressive illness as treatable medical diseases; to foster self-help for patients and families; to eliminate discrimination and stigma; to improve access to care; and to advocate for research toward the elimination of these illnesses.

Families & Youth, Inc.
1320 S. Solano Dr.
Las Cruces, NM 88001
Phone: (505) 522-4004
Type of organization: Multi-setting mental-health organizations.

New Mexico Behavioral Health Services Division
1190 Saint Francis Dr., Room N. 3300
Santa Fe, NM 87502
Phone: (505) 827-2601; (800) 362-2013
Fax: (505) 827-0097
URL: www.nmcares.org/
Type of organization: State mental-health agency.

Sequoyah Adolescent Treatment Center
3405 W. Pan American Fwy. N.E.
Albuquerque, NM 87107
Phone: (505) 344-4673
Type of organization: Residential treatment centers for children.

University of New Mexico Children's Psychiatric Hospital
1001 Yale Blvd. N.E.
Albuquerque, NM 87131

Phone: (505) 272-2890
Type of organization: Public psychiatric hospitals.

New York

Action for Mental Health
1585 Kenmore Ave.
Kenmore, NY 14217
Phone: (716) 871-0581
Fax: (716) 871-0614
Type of organization: Action for Mental Health is a consumer-based agency serving Erie County. It provides advocacy, civic education and training, and develops self-help groups to empower consumers of mental health services.

Behavioral Health Services North, Inc.
159 Margaret St., Suite 201
Plattsburgh, NY 12901
Phone: (518) 563-8206; (518) 563-8207
Fax: (518) 563-9958
URL: www.bhsn.org

Children & Family MH Services
37 John St.
Amityville, NY 11701-2930
Phone: (631) 264-4325
Type of organization: Outpatient clinics.

St. Catherine's Center for Children
40 N. Main Ave.
Albany, NY 12203
Phone: (518) 453-6700
Type of organization: Residential treatment centers for children.

St. Mary's Hospital
Children's Mental Health Clinic
380 Guy Park Ave.
Amsterdam, NY 12010
Phone: (518) 841-7453
Type of organization: General hospitals with separate psychiatric units.

North Carolina

Crossroads Behavioral Healthcare
200 Business Park Dr.
Elkin, NC 28621
Phone: (336) 835-1000
Type of organization: Residential treatment centers for children.

Crossroads Behavioral Healthcare
385 Timber Road
Mooresville, NC 28115
Phone: (704) 660-1020
Type of organization: Residential treatment centers for children.

Mental Health Association—Forsyth County
1509 S. Hawthorne Road
Winston-Salem, NC 27103
Phone: (336) 768-3880
Fax: (336) 768-3505
URL: www.mha-fc.org
Type of organization: The Mental Health Association provides services and information on mental and emotional problems and makes referrals to resources for help. The association has an onsite resource center.

Mental Health Association of Orange County
PO Box 2253
Chapel Hill, NC 27515
Phone: (919) 942-8083
URL: www.mhaoc.com
Type of organization: Affiliate of the North Carolina Mental Health Association. Promotes positive mental health among citizens of Orange County through advocacy, collaboration, education, and services.

North Dakota

Mental Health Association of North Dakota
P O Box 4106
Bismarck, ND 58502
Phone: (479) 255-3692

Fax: (479) 255-2411
Type of organization: State affiliate of the NMHA.

North Dakota Division of Mental Health and Substance Abuse Services
600 S. 2nd St., Suite 1D
Bismarck, ND 58504
Phone: (800) 755-2719; (701) 328-8940
Fax: (701) 328-8969
URL: lnotes.state.nd.us/dhs/dhsweb.nsf/ServicePages/MentalHealthand SubstanceAbuseServices
Type of organization: State mental-health agency.

The Village Family Service Center (North Dakota)
1201 25th St. S.
Fargo, ND 58103
Phone: (701) 451-4900
URL: www.thevillagefamily.org
Type of organization: The Village provides a full range of services including counseling programs, adoption, financial counseling, and mentoring programs such as the Big Brother Big Sister Program. The Village has 20 offices throughout North Dakota and Minnesota. Thanks to United Way and donor support, The Village services are available at a reduced fee for eligible participants.

Ohio

Child and Adolescent Service Center
919 Second St. N.E.
Canton, OH 44704
Phone: (800) 791-7917; (330) 454-7917
Fax: (330) 454-1476
Type of organization: The center provides mental-health services for children and adolescents, family counseling, group therapy, individual counseling, and psychological services.

Eastway Behavioral Corporation
Community Living Center
2831 Salem Ave.
Dayton, OH 45406

Phone: (937) 276-4167
Type of organization: Residential treatment centers for children.

Thompkins Child & Adolescent Services
2007 E. Wheeling Ave.
Cambridge, OH 43725
Phone: (740) 432-2377
Type of organization: Residential treatment centers for children.

Oklahoma

Family and Children Services
3604 N. Cinncati
Tulsa, OK 74106
Phone: (918) 425-4200
Type of organization: Outpatient that deals with children and adolescents with mental illnesses.

Federation of Families for Children's Mental Health
P.O. Box 50370
Tulsa, OK 74150
Phone: (918) 224-3476
Type of organization: Family support group that offers advocacy and education to families with children that have behavioral or emotional disorders or mental illness.

Oklahoma Department of Mental Health and Substance Abuse Services
P.O. Box 53277
Capital Station
Oklahoma City, OK 73152
Phone: (800) 522-9054; (405) 522-3908
Domestic Violence Safeline: (800) 522-7233
Fax: (405) 522-3650
URL: www.odmhsas.org
Type of organization: State mental-health agency.

Oklahoma Youth Center
320 12th Ave. N.E.
Norman, OK 73071

Phone: (405) 573-2222
Type of organization: Residential treatment centers for children.

Oklahoma Youth Center
320 12th Avenue North East
Norman, OK 73071
Type of organization: Sate-run facility for children and adolescents with mental illness.

Oregon

Morrison Center Child & Family Services
Behavior Intervention Center
5205 S.E. 86th Ave.
Portland, OR 97266
Phone: (503) 916-5590
Type of organization: Residential treatment centers for children.

NAMI Oregon
2620 Greenway Dr. N.E.
Salem, OR 97301
Phone: (800) 343-6264; (503) 370-7774
Fax: (503) 370-9452
URL: www.namioregon.org
Type of organization: NAMI Oregon is a support and advocacy organization. It sponsors local support groups and offers education and information about community services for people with mental illness and their families.

Oregon Department of Mental Health
500 Summer St. N.E., E86
Salem, OR 97301
Phone: (503) 945-5763
Fax: (503) 378-8467
URL: www.dhs.state.or.us/mentalhealth/
Type of organization: Assures that the rights of people with mental illness are protected. Assists counties and other providers in the delivery of services. Assures the provision of services close to home, as early as possible, and in the most normal setting to allow an adequate level of indepen-

dence and to avoid disruption in the person's life. Assures effective care, treatment, and training in secure facilities or closely supervised programs for persons with mental illness who exhibit dangerous behavior.

Research and Training Center on Family Support and Children's Mental Health
Portland State University
P.O. Box 751
Portland, OR 97207
Phone: (503) 725-4040
Fax: (503) 725-4180
URL: www.rtc.pdx.edu
Type of organization: The Research and Training Center on Family Support and Children's Mental Health conducts research on the child mental-health service system and provides training and technical assistance to individuals and organizations working on behalf of children with emotional and/or behavioral disorders. The center's activities are based on the tenets of the Comprehensive Service System model, which stresses the importance of community based, family centered, and culturally appropriate services for children and their families.

Pennsylvania

Children's Service Center
Mental Health Group Home
137 E. Noble St.
Nanticoke, PA 18634
Phone: (570) 735-7369
Type of organization: Residential treatment centers for children.

DBSA Friends for Friends
4641 Roosevelt Blvd.
Philadelphia, PA 19124
Phone: (215) 831-7809
Fax: (610) 525-3832
Type of organization: Educate patients, families, and professionals, and the public concerning the nature of depressive and manic-depressive illness as treatable medical diseases; to foster self-help for patients and families; to

eliminate discrimination and stigma; to improve access to care; and to advocate for research toward the elimination of these illnesses.

Horizon House, Inc.
120 S. 30th St.
Philadelphia, PA 19104
Phone: (215) 386-3838
Fax: (215) 382-3626
Type of organization: Provides an environment in which individuals with mental-health needs, developmental disabilities, homelessness, and substance-abuse problems can develop the skills necessary to enjoy rewarding lives. Offers assessment/outpatient services, day programs, partial hospitalization, vocational services, education, social rehabilitation, homeless services, substance-abuse services, specialized residential, intensive case management, developmental, and suburban.

KidsPeace National Centers
1650 Broadway
Bethlehem, PA 18015
Phone: (800) 8KID-123
URL: www.kidspeace.org
Type of organization: The national referral network for kids in crisis. KidsPeace is dedicated to serving the critical behavioral and mental-health needs of children, preadolescents, and teens. Operates in 10 states: Pennsylvania, New York, Indiana, Maine, Maryland, New Jersey, Minnesota, Georgia, North Carolina, and Virginia.

Tioga County Dept of Human Services
Clinical Services
149 E. Main St.
Knoxville, PA 16928
Phone: (814) 326-4680
Type of organization: Residential treatment centers for children.

Rhode Island

Blackstone Adolescent Counseling Center
Community Counseling Center
475 Fountain St.
Pawtucket, RI 02860

Phone: (401) 724-0535
Type of organization: Residential treatment centers for children.

Blackstone Children's Home
Community Counseling Center
50 Walcott St.
Pawtucket, RI 02860
Phone: (401) 729-1516
Type of organization: Residential treatment centers for children.

Mental Health Association of Rhode Island
500 Prospect St.
Pawtucket, RI 02860
Phone: (401) 726-8383
Fax: (401) 365-6170
URL: www.mhari.org
Type of organization: Affiliate of the NMHA.

NAMI Rhode Island
1255 N. Main St.
Providence, RI 02904
Phone: (800) 749-3197; (401) 331-3060
Fax: (401) 274-3020
URL: ri.nami.org/
Type of organization: NAMI Rhode Island is a support and advocacy organization. It sponsors local support groups and offers education and information about community services for people with mental illness and their families.

Parent Support Network
400 Warwick Ave., Suite 12
Warwick, RI 02888
Phone: (800) 483-8844; (401) 467-6855
Fax: (401) 467-6903
Type of organization: The Parent Support Network is an organization of families supporting families with children and youths who are at risk for or have behavioral or emotional challenges. Its goals are to: strengthen and preserve families; enable families in self-advocacy; extend social networks and reduce family isolation; and develop social policy and systems of care. The Parent Support Network accomplishes these goals by providing advocacy,

education and training, promoting outreach and public awareness, facilitating social events for families, and participating on committees responsible for developing, implementing, and evaluating policies and systems of care.

Rhode Island Department of Mental Health, Mental Retardation, and Hospitals
14 Harrington Road, Barry Hall
Cranston, RI 02920
Phone: (401) 462-3201
Fax: (401) 462-3204
URL: www.mhrh.state.ri.us

Valley Community School-Middletown
Community Counseling Center
60 Hammarlund Way
Middletown, RI 02842
Phone: (401) 849-6981
Type of organization: Residential treatment centers for children. State mental-health agency.

South Carolina

The National Alliance for the Mentally Ill
Maintains a helpline for information on mental illnesses and referrals to local groups. The local self-help groups have support and advocacy components and offer education and information about community services for families and individuals. For information about the alliance's affiliates and activities in your state, contact:
NAMI South Carolina
P.O. Box 1267
Columbia, SC 29202
Phone: (803) 733-9592; (800) 788-5131
Fax: (803) 733-9591
E-mail: namiofsc@logicsouth.com
URL: www.namisc.org

Piedmont Center for Mental Health Services
Clear Spring Home
108 Clear Spring Road
Simpsonville, SC 29681

Phone: (864) 967-4432
Type of organization: Residential treatment centers for children.

Piedmont Center for Mental Health Services
Greer Mental Health Clinic
220 Executive Dr.
Greer, SC 29651
Phone: (864) 879-2111
Type of organization: Residential treatment centers for children.

Piedmont Center for Mental Health Services
Rainbow House/Day Program
900 W. Poinsett St.
Greer, SC 29650
Phone: (864) 879-1088
Type of organization: Residential treatment centers for children.

South Carolina Department of Mental Health
P.O. Box 485
2414 Bull St.
Columbia, SC 29202
Phone: (803) 898-8581
Fax: (803) 898-8316
URL: www.state.sc.us/dmh
Type of organization: State mental-health agency.

South Dakota

South Dakota Division of Mental Health
Hillsview Plaza, E. Hwy 34
c/o 500 E. Capitol
Pierre, SD 57501
Phone: (800) 265-9684; (605) 773-5991
Fax: (605) 773-7076
URL: www.state.sd.us/dhs/dmh/
Type of organization: State mental-health agency.

Southeastern Behavioral HealthCare
Canton Office
112 1/2 S. Broadway St.
Canton, SD 57013

Phone: (605) 987-2561
Type of organization: Residential treatment centers for children.

Southeastern Behavioral HealthCare
Parker Office
400 S. Main St.
Parker, SD 57053
Phone: (605) 297-3699
Type of organization: Residential treatment centers for children.

Southeastern Behavioral HealthCare
Salem Office
121 N. Main St.
Salem, SD 57058
Phone: (605) 425-2165
Type of organization: Residential treatment centers for children.

State Mental-Health Agency
For more information about admission, care, treatment, release, and patient follow-up in public or private psychiatric residential facilities, contact:
Kim Malsam-Rysdon, Director
Division of Mental Health
Department of Human Services
Hillsview Plaza, East Highway 34
c/o 500 East Capitol
Pierre, SD 57501-5070
Phone: 605-773-5991; (800) 265-9684
Fax: 605-773-7076

Tennessee

Child & Family Tennessee
Therapeutic Visitation
901 E. Summit Hill Dr.
Knoxville, TN 37915
Phone: (865) 521-5640
Type of organization: Residential treatment centers for children.

Mental Health Association (I&R)—Memphis
1407 Union Ave., Suite 1205
Memphis, TN 38104
Phone: (901) 323-0633
Fax: (901) 323-0858
Type of organization: Offers information and referrals to local support groups. Provides public education and information forums on issues related to mental health, professional training and seminars, as well as assistance in starting new groups and consultation to existing groups. Also offers facilitator training and speakers bureau.

Tennessee Association of Mental-Health Organizations (TAMHO)
42 Rutledge St.
Nashville, TN 37210
Phone: (800) 568-2642; (615) 244-2220
Fax: (615) 254-8331
URL: www.tamho.org
Type of organization: TAMHO is a nonprofit organization of community mental-health organizations in the state of Tennessee. Their mission is to improve the mental-health care system in the state. It offers an opportunity for member agencies to network, and publish the "TAMHO Membership Directory and Buyer's Guide."

Tennessee Voices for Children
1315 8th Ave. S.
Nashville, TN 37203
Phone: (800) 670-9882; (615) 269-7751
Fax: (615) 269-8914
URL: www.tnvoices.org
Type of organization: Family support organization.

Texas

American Society for Adolescent Psychiatry
P.O. Box 570218
Dallas, TX 75357
Phone: (972) 686-6166

Fax: (972) 613-5532
URL: www.adolpsych.org
Type of organization: ASAP supports research and provides a source of informed psychiatric opinion on adolescents. Members are psychiatrists with either a specialty or an active interest in adolescent psychiatry. ASAP conducts seminars and conferences. It is supported by dues.

Betty Hardwick Center
Adult & Youth Outpatient/Crisis Services
2626 S. Clack St.
Abilene, TX 79606
Phone: (325) 690-5100
Type of organization: Outpatient clinics.

Child & Family Guidance Center
8915 Harry Hines Blvd.
Dallas, TX 75235
Phone: (214) 351-3490
Type of organization: Outpatient clinics.

Dallas Federation of Families for Children's Mental Health
2629 Sharpview Lane
Dallas, TX 75228
Phone: (214) 320-1825
Fax: (214) 320-3750
Type of organization: The Dallas Federation is an advocacy service for families in need. They act as a liaison between professionals and families in need of specialized services for children with emotional/behavioral problems. It conducts trainings and workshops on national, state and local levels, regarding children's mental health.

Depressive and Manic Depressive Association—Amarillo/ Panhandle
1605 Parker St.
Amarillo, TX 79102
Phone: (806) 372-1023
Type of organization: Educate patients, families, and professionals, and the public concerning the nature of depressive and manic-depressive illness as treatable medical diseases; to foster self-help for patients and families; to eliminate discrimination and stigma; to improve access to care; and to advocate for research toward the elimination of these illnesses.

Utah

The Information and Referral Center—Salt Lake City
1025 S. 700 W.
Salt Lake City, UT 84104
Phone: (801) 978-3333
Fax: (801) 978-9565
URL: www.informationandreferral.org
Type of organization: Provides information and referral to local self-help groups in select areas. Also provides information on other local services and agencies.

Wasatch Mental Health Center
Heber City Office
135 S. Main, Suite 206
Heber City, UT 84032
Phone: (435) 654-1618
Type of organization: Residential treatment centers for children.

Wasatch Mental Health Center
Residential Supportive
750 North Freedom Blvd.
Provo, UT 84601
Phone: (801) 489-8045
Type of organization: Residential treatment centers for children.

Wasatch Mental Health Youth Services
Park View School
1161 E. 300 N.
Provo, UT 84606
Phone: (801) 373-4765
Type of organization: Residential treatment centers for children.

Vermont

Brookhaven Home for Boys Inc.
331 Main St.
Chelsea, VT 05038
Phone: (802) 685-4458
Type of organization: Residential treatment centers for children.

Howard Center for Human Services
Baird Center for Children & Families
1110 Pine St.
Burlington, VT 05401
Phone: (802) 863-1326
Type of organization: Multi-setting mental-health organizations.

Laraway Youth and Family Services
Laraway School, Inc.
PO Box 621
Johnson, VT 05656
Phone: (802) 635-2805
Type of organization: Residential treatment centers for children.

Vermont Association for Mental Health
P.O. Box 165
Montpelier, VT 05601
Phone: (802) 223-6263; (800) 639-4052
Fax: (802) 828-5252
URL: www.vamh.org
Type of organization: Vermont chapter of the National Mental Health Association. Advocates for children and adults with psychiatric disabilities or substance abuse problems.

Vermont Division of Developmental and Mental Health Services
The Weeks Bldg.
103 S. Main St.
Waterbury, VT 05671
Phone: (888) 212-4677; (802) 241-2610
Fax: (802) 241-1129
URL: www.state.vt.us/dmh/
Type of organization: State mental-health agency.

Vermont Federation of Families for Children's Mental Health
P.O. Box 607
Montpelier, VT 05601
Phone: (800) 639-6071
Fax: (802) 828-2159
Type of organization: Parent-advocacy group for families with children that have mental-health-care needs.

Virginia

Bridges Child & Adolescent Treatment Center
693 Leesville Road
Lynchburg, VA 24502
Phone: (434) 947-5700
Type of organization: Residential treatment centers for children.

Federation of Families for Children's Mental Health
1101 King St., Suite 420
Alexandria, VA 22314
Phone: (703) 684-7710
Fax: (703) 836-1040
URL: www.ffcmh.org
Type of organization: The federation is a national advocacy and support organization for families of children with mental, emotional, or behavioral disorders. It sponsors parent-advocacy groups across the country where parents can find support and learn about the children's mental-health system and services in their community. The federation advocates for services on the national, state, and local levels, and promotes family involvement in the mental-health system. It sponsors an annual conference and publishes a newsletter.

International Mental Health Association Information Center
2001 N. Beauregard St., 12th Floor
Alexandria, VA 22311
Phone: (703) 684-7722; (800) 969-6642
TDD: (800) 433-5959
Fax: (703) 684-5968
E-mail: infoctr@nmha.org
URL: www.nmha.org; www.state.sd.us/dhs/dmh
Type of organization: MHAF is a nonprofit organization dedicated to addressing all aspects of mental health and mental illness through advocacy, education, and support services.

Mental Health Association in Fredericksburg
2217 Princess Anne St., Suite 219-1
Fredericksburg, VA 22401

Phone: (800) 684-6423; (540) 371-2704
Fax: (540) 372-3709
URL: www.fls.infi.net/~mhaf

National Mental Health Association Information Center
2001 N. Beauregard St., 12th Floor
Alexandria, VA 22311
Phone: (703) 684-7722; (800) 969-6642
(TDD) 800-433-5959
Fax: 703-684-5968
E-mail: infoctr@nmha.org
URL: www.nmha.org
Type of organization: The National Alliance for the Mentally Ill maintains a helpline for information on mental illnesses and referrals to local groups. The local self-help groups have support and advocacy components and offer education and information about community services for families and individuals.

Whisper Ridge Behavioral Health System
2101 Arlington Blvd.
Charlottesville, VA 22903
Phone: (434) 977-1523
Type of organization: Residential treatment centers for children.

Washington

Department of Social and Health Services
P.O. Box 45320
Olympia, WA 98504
Phone: (800) 446-0259; (360) 902-0790
Fax: (360) 902-0809
URL: www.wa.gov/dshs/
Type of organization: State mental-health agency.

Ryther Child Center
2400 N.E. 95th St.
Seattle, WA 98115
Phone: (206) 525-5050

Fax: (206) 525-9795
URL: www.ryther.org
Type of organization: Ryther Child Center offers safe places for children to heal and grow in residential settings and homes. Ryther helps children achieve better lives through high quality and intensive mental health and chemical dependence services with compassionate concern for each child. These services are provided by an energetic, devoted staff of highly trained professionals and skilled child-care workers committed to continuous improvement and enhancement of the Ryther continuum of care.

State Mental-Health Agency
For more information about admission, care, treatment, release, and patient follow-up in public or private psychiatric residential facilities, contact your state mental-health agency:
Karl Brimner, Director
Mental Health Division
Department of Social and Health Services
P.O. Box 45320
Olympia, WA 98504
Phone: 360-902-8070; (800) 446-0259 (statewide)
Fax: 360-902-0809
URL: www1.dshs.wa.gov/mentalhealth/

Washington State Office of Children with Special Health Care Needs
Office of Maternal & Child Health
Department of Health
New Market Industrial Bldg., 10
P.O. Box 47835
Olympia, WA 98504
Phone: (360) 236-3571
URL: www.doh.wa.gov/cfh/mch/CSHCNhome2.htm
Type of organization: The Children with Special Health Care Needs (CSHCN) program services children who have serious physical, behavioral, or emotional conditions that require health and related services beyond those generally required by children.

West Virginia

Family Support

The Center for Mental Health Services awards grants to statewide, family-run networks to provide support and information to families of children and adolescents with serious emotional, behavioral, or mental disorders. For more information, contact:

Terri Toothman, Executive Director
Mountain State Parents, Children & Adolescent Network
P.O. Box 6658
Wheeling, WV 26003
Phone: 304-233-5399; 800-244-5385 (statewide)
Fax: 304-233-3847
E-mail: ttoothman@mspcan.org
URL: www.mspcan.org

Mountain State Parents Can
Children and Adolescent Network
P.O. Box 6658
Wheeling, WV 26003
Phone: (800) 244-5385
URL: www.mspcan.org

The Region II Family Network
940 4th Ave., Suite 321
Huntington, WV 25701
Phone: 888-711-4334
E-mail: MSFA2003@aol.com

Wisconsin

Alliance for Children and Families
11700 W. Lake Park Dr.
Milwaukee, WI 53224
Phone: (800) 221-3726; (414) 359-1040
Fax: (414) 359-1074
URL: www.alliance1.org/
Type of organization: The Alliance for Children and Families represents more than 350 child-and family-service organizations. The alliance formed

in 1998 after the merging of Family Service America and the National Association of Homes and Services for Children.

Depression & Bipolar Support Alliance of SE Wisconsin
P.O. Box 13306
Milwaukee, WI 53213
Phone: (414) 964-2586
Type of organization: Self-help support group for individuals 17 and older who have depression, bipolar disorder or related illnesses. Services are extended to family and friends and include education and support in an atmosphere of confidentiality and trust, and shared experiences. Meetings are on the first and third Monday of every month from 10–11:30 A.M., and the second and fourth Monday from 7–9 P.M. Wheelchair accessible, but call ahead for elevator services.

Northwest System
Northwest Counseling & Guidance Clinic
203 United Way
Frederic, WI 54837
Phone: (715) 327-4402
Type of organization: Residential treatment centers for children.

State Protection and Advocacy Agency
Each state has a protection and advocacy agency that receives funding from the Federal Center for Mental Health Services. Agencies are mandated to protect and advocate for the rights of people with mental illnesses and to investigate reports of abuse and neglect in facilities that care for or treat individuals with mental illnesses. These facilities, which may be public or private, include hospitals, nursing homes, community facilities, board and care homes, homeless shelters, jails, and prisons. Agencies provide advocacy services or conduct investigations to address issues that arise during transportation or admission to such facilities, during residency in them, or within 90 days after discharge from them. Contact:
Wisconsin Coalition for Advocacy, Inc.
16 North Carroll St., Suite 400
Madison, WI 53703
Phone/TDD: 608-267-0214; 800-928-8778 (statewide, consumers and family members only)
Fax: (608) 267-0368
URL: www.w-c-a.org

We Are the Children's Hope
2943 N. 9th St.
Milwaukee, WI 53206
Phone: (414) 263-3375
Fax: (414) 263-1148
Type of organization: Parent-advocacy group.

Wyoming

Family Support
The Center for Mental Health Services awards grants to statewide, family-run networks to provide support and information to families of children and adolescents with serious emotional, behavioral, or mental disorders. For more information, contact:
Peggy Nikkel, Executive Director
UPLIFT
P.O. Box 664
Cheyenne, WY 82003
Phone: (307) 778-8686; (888) UPLIFT-3 (875-4383)
Fax: (307) 778-8681
URL: www.upliftwy.org

NAMI Wyoming
P.O. Box 165
Torrington, WY 82240
Phone: (307) 532-3290
Fax: (307) 532-3290
URL: www.wyami.org
Type of organization: NAMI Wyoming is a support and advocacy organization. It sponsors local support groups and offers education and information about community services for people with mental illness and their families.

Wyoming Department of Health: Mental Health Division
6101 Yellowstone Road, Room 259-B
Cheyenne, WY 82002
Phone: (307) 777-7997
Fax: (307) 777-5580
URL: mentalhealth.state.wy.us/
Type of organization: State mental-health agency.

References

Adler, J. (1998, September 14). Online and bummed out. *Newsweek*, *132*(11), 84.

American Academy of Child and Adolescent Psychiatry, (2005). The use of medication in treating childhood and adolescent depression: Information for patients and families. Retrieved June 1, 2005, from http://ParentsMedGuide.org.

Anderson, J. C., & McGee, R. (1994). Comorbidity of depression in children and adolescents. In W. M. Reynolds & H. F. Johnson (Eds.), *Handbook of depression in children and adolescents* (pp. 581–601). New York: Plenum.

Angold, A., & Costello, E. J. (1993). Depressive comorbidity in children and adolescents: Empirical, theoretical, and methodological issues. *American Journal of Psychiatry*, *150*, 1774–1791.

Beck, A. T. (1967). *Depression, clinical, experimental, and theoretical aspects.* New York: Hoeber.

Beck, A. (1987). *Cognitive therapy of depression*. New York: Guilford Press.

Birmaher et al. (1996). Childhood and adolescent depression: A review of the past 10 years. *Journal of the American Academy of Child and Adolescent Psychiatry*, *35*, 1427–1439.

Centers for Disease Control and Prevention. (2005). National Center for Health Statistics, Parental report of emotional and behavioral difficulties. Retrieved October 17, 2005, from http://childstats.ed.gov.

Dumont, R., & Rauch, M. (2000). Test review: Scale for assessing emotional disturbance (SAED). *Online Journal of Communique*, *28*(8), 24–25. Retrieved June 3, 2005, from http://alpha.fdu.edu/psychology/SAED.htm.

Fitzpatrick, C., & Sharry, J. (2004). *Coping with depression in young people: A guide for parents.* West Sussex, England: John Wiley & Sons.

Friedrich, W., Jacobs, J., & Reams, R. (1982). Depression and suicidal ideation in early adolescents. *Journal of Youth and Adolescence*, *11*, 403–407.

Garrison, C. Z., Walker, J. L., Cuffee, S. P., Mckeown, R. E., Addy, C. L., & Jackson, K. L. (1997). Incidence of major depressive disorder and dysthymia in young adolescents. *Journal of the American Academy of Child and Adolescent Psychiatry*, *36*, 458–465.

Hersen, M., & Ollendick, T. H. (1993). *The handbook of child and adolescent assessment.* Boston: Allyn and Bacon.

Kessler, R. C., Walters, E. E., & Forthofer, M. S. (1998, August). The social consequences of psychiatric disorders III: Probability of marital stability. *American Journal of Psychiatry*, *155*, 1092–1096.

Kovacs, M. (1996). Presentation and course of major depressive disorder during childhood and later years of the life span. *Journal of the American Academy of Child and Adolescent Psychiatry*, *35*(6), 705–715.

Magg, J. W., & Behrens, J. T. (1989). Depression and cognitive self-statements of learning disabled and seriously disturbed adolescents. *Journal of Special Education*, *23*, 17–27.

Magg, J. W., Behrens, J. T., & DiGangi, S. A. (1991). Dysfunctional cognitions associated with adolescent depression. *Child and Family Behavior Therapy*, *10*, 29–47.

National Institute of Mental Health. (2003). Depression. Retrieved October 23, 2005, from www.nimh.nih.gov.publicat/depression.cfm.

National Institute of Mental Health. (2005). Depression in children and adolescents. Retrieved July 15, 2005, from http://www.nimh.nih.gov/healthinformation/depchildmenu.cfm.

Psychological Publications, Inc. (2004). Children's depression inventory. Retrieved October 13, 2005, from www.tjta.com.

Raeburn, R. (2003). Acquainted with the night: A parent's quest to understand depression and bipolar disorder in his children. Retrieved June 3, 2005, from http://www.nimh.nih.gov.

Regier, D. A., Narrow, W. E., Rae, D. S., Manderscheid, R. W., Locke, B. Z., & Goodwin, F. K. (1993). The defacto U.S. mental and addictive disorders service system: Epidemiologic catchment area prospective one year prevalence rates of disorders and services. *Archives of General Psychiatry*, *50*, 85–94.

Reynolds,W. M., & Coats, K. L. (1986). A comparison of cognitive behavioral therapy and relaxation training for the treatment of depression in adolescents. *Journal of Consulting and Clinical Psychology*, *54*, 653–660.

Reynolds,W. M., & Kobak, K. A. (1996). Reynolds Depression Screening Inventory (RDSI). Retrieved June 1, 2005, from www.ascs4help.com/testing/personcounsel/rdsi.htm.

Shaffer, D., & Craft, L. (1999). Methods of adolescent suicide prevention. *Journal of Clinical Psychiatry*, *60*, 70–74.

Shaughnessy, M. (1998). The emotionally sensitive adolescent report. Retrieved October 23, 2006, from http://www.ed.gov/index.jhtml.

Smucker, M. R., Craighead, W. E., Craighead, L. W., & Green, B. J. (1986). Normative and reliability data for the children's depression inventory. *Journal of Abnormal Child Psychology*, *14*, 25–39.

U.S. Department of Health and Human Services. (1999). Depression and suicide in children and adolescents. Retrieved October 17, 2005, from http://www.surgeongeneral.gov/library/mentalhealth/chapter3/sec5.html.

Voelker, R. (2003). Researchers probe depression in children. *Journal of the American Medical Association*, *289*, 3078–3079.

Wirt, A., Lachar D., Klinedinst, B., & Seat, M. (1983).The personality inventory for children. Los Angeles: Western Psychological Services.

Zeman, S. (1996, August). Causes of depression. *Prospect Magazine*, 11. Retrieved October 12, 2005, from www.prospect-magazine.co.uk.